William Styron's
Sophie's Choice
Crime and Self-Punishment

by
Rhoda Sirlin

With a Foreword by
William Styron

 Research
Press

Ann Arbor / London

Produced and distributed by
UMI Research Press
an imprint of
University Microfilms Inc.
Ann Arbor, Michigan 48106

Library of Congress Cataloging in Publication Data

Sirlin, Rhoda.
   William Styron's Sophie's choice : crime and self-punish-
ment / by Rhoda Sirlin ; with a foreword by William Styron.
   p. cm.—(Challenging the literary canon)
   Includes bibliographical references and index.
   ISBN 0-8357-2043-8 (alk. paper)
   1. Styron, William, 1952- Sophie's choice. 2. World War,
1939-1945—Literature and the war. 3. Auschwitz (Poland :
Concentration camp) in literature. I. Title. II. Series.
PS3569.T9S6737   1990
813'.54—dc20   89-20458
                                                          CIP

British Library CIP data is available.

The paper used in this publication meets the minimum requirements of
American National Standard for Information Sciences—Permanence of Paper
for Printed Library Materials, ANSI Z39.48-1984. ∞ ™

William Styron's
Sophie's Choice
Crime and Self-Punishment

Challenging the Literary Canon

To the memory of
Charles Child Walcutt
(1908–1989)
and
James Smith
(1922–1988)

Contents

Foreword

There were three bothersome caveats which haunted me before and during the writing of *Sophie's Choice*. All three of these admonishments, deriving from the conventional wisdom of that period—the mid and late 1970s—had to do with certain fixed ideas about Auschwitz, and were calculated to defeat all but the most resolute novelist from attempting to write a book like the one I had set out to complete. While none of them caused me anything much more than a brief hesitation, I must confess that there were times when I did regard them seriously, and they are worth citing here a decade later.

First, one should not write about Auschwitz at all. "There can be no poetry after Auschwitz," wrote Theodor Adorno in a famous statement whose magisterial resonance seems to grow somewhat hollow with the passage of time. This plea for silence in the face of the awesome fact of the extermination of millions of people began to gain attention at along about the time I was writing *Sophie's Choice;* it was a viewpoint most notably present in the essays of George Steiner and Elie Wiesel (both of whom have remained far from silent), and it troubled me enough so that I felt compelled to address myself to the question within the body of my novel, at the beginning of chapter 9. There I resolved the argument to my own satisfaction, at least, with reasons that seem just as valid to me now as when I first set them down. In fact, I now believe I might have been a bit too timid and reserved in expressing myself. For it would seem at this moment that there is at the very least an element of sanctimony in this appeal for silence. What is there dwelling intrinsically in the fact of Auschwitz, after all, which renders it out of bounds to the artist in honest quest of its essence? Granted that it is a catastrophe of unparalleled dimension in history manifesting an enormity so appalling that we are almost forced to invent a new vocabulary to encompass its meaning. Still, once this is recognized, what is there so sacrosanct about Auschwitz that a writer should be prevented from trying to grasp its significance? Since no response comes readily to mind, one must conclude that a certain overblown rhetoric is at the heart of the prohibition. It seems to me that no subject can be placed beyond the purview of the artist, at least one who approaches his task with the respect and reverence which Auschwitz by its very nature demands.

The second warning concerned Auschwitz as a legitimate topic for any writer who had not himself been a survivor. If you had not been there you had no right to deal with it. This certainly did give me serious pause from time to time, since clearly even the boldest novelist, fully aware of the risks he is taking, cannot help feeling daunted when he intrudes on the experience which belongs to others; there is a sense of being a usurper of others' emotions, not to mention their suffering. Yet once again the chief question would appear to be not whether the writer has the the right to do this—his right is beyond dispute—but whether his imagination, combined with his fidelity to historical truth, is capable of creating an artful and convincing work of literature, irrespective of his own personal connection with the subject. And once more, the proscription against the outsider attempting to grapple with the mystery of Auschwitz strikes me as empty piety. If we denied the outsider the right to deal with events which had not impinged directly on his own life we would have eliminated a vast amount of literature, especially historical works, including Tolstoy and Dickens. This is not to disregard the special sensibility needed to write of Auschwitz, and in creating *Sophie's Choice* I was constantly aware of the hazards. I sensed an infringement, almost an indecency, on my part should I dare to try to delineate the core of the concentration camp, with its tortures and personal indignities, its unspeakable barbarities. And therefore I deliberately distanced myself from the interior of Auschwitz, setting all of the action outside of the camp, in the Commandant's house, where the horrors could be registered through Sophie's consciousness as remote—albeit not-too-remote—sights, sounds and smells. If this strategy succeeded it was doubtless due to the discretion I felt I had to display in being *near* Auschwitz and its atrocities, but not *of* them; yet plainly it was necessary to disregard the admonition that as one who had not been there I had no right to deal with Auschwitz at all.

Finally, there was my concern about writing of an event and symbol which to a singular degree—at least in the popular mind—have become the property of Jews. The Sophie I based my heroine on was a real character in my life; though her "choice" was an imagined happening, the Sophie I knew had suffered cruelly at Auschwitz and had been a Catholic. Therefore, a certain deterministic logic helped prevent me in my fiction from converting her to a Jew. Still, I was aware of the harsh criticism I might receive by making a non-Jew, so centrally positioned in the story, a sacrificial victim. Even in the late 1970s, when a public consciousness of the Holocaust was just gaining momentum, there was often caustic mention of writers and artists "universalizing" the event by permitting non-Jews—Poles and other Slavs, Gypsies—to be portrayed as suffering the same fate as the Jews. This view seemed to me then as now proprietary in the extreme; if at Auschwitz—to give but one example—thirty to thirty-five percent of the dead were Slavs or Gypsies, dying not so systematically as the Jews but in the end just as decisively, then their loss and their agony should be placed into the equation. If anyone wished, then, to construe Sophie as a symbolic martyr of this vast "other" population, he would have the historical record to validate his impression. But those who have insisted on viewing Sophie as ill-chosen, a false metaphor for the victimization of which Jews were the chief recipients at Auschwitz, should consider why I felt compelled, as an artist, to make the decisions I did. First, to have made Sophie Jewish would have been to create "a banal character"—it was a rabbi, of all people, who made this comment to me in a letter shortly after the book was published. What he was saying to me was, I believe, what I was trying in effect to say in literary terms: the entire world knows by now the horrors inflicted on the Jews. What then, indeed, about the suffering of these others? But even this is less important to me than the way Sophie, through her father and his anti-Semitism, represents the victim of the wheel of evil which comes full circle. It is his doctrine, after all, which crushes his innocent daughter and his even more innocent grandchildren with a lethal finality; their deaths are really the product of his hatred of the Jews. Such sublime hatred will eventually destroy everyone—Jew and Christian, even one's own flesh. It is a puzzle to me how this aspect of the story has escaped those critics who have seen in my "universalizing" of Auschwitz an affront to the Jewish people.

In the present volume, Rhoda Sirlin has, I think, addressed with great skill and sensitivity these and other matters which are contained in *Sophie's Choice.* Her insights are especially valuable insofar as they deal with the areas of contention I have mentioned. For *Sophie's Choice* has attracted a fair amount of heated controversy. It did not receive the onslaught of criticism, some of it quite hysterical and venomous, that came in the wake of the publication of *The Confessions of Nat Turner* in 1967. Indeed, given the volatile nature of the subject matter and the way in which a growing awareness of the Holocaust coincided with the publication of *Sophie's Choice,* I was a little surprised by the relatively scant controversy which attended its appearance in the summer of 1979. Yet as time passed I began to hear echoes of violent dissent from certain quarters, and it has become clear to me that for some people—those who view the Holocaust from a rigid perspective—*Sophie's Choice* is considered distinctly *non grata.* It is not the novelist's task to dissuade people from the prejudices and the preconceived fallacies that cluster around his book; if he has hewn to his vision with passion and fidelity to the truth as he sees it, he will have perhaps done all he needs to. Much of the scholar's task, on the other hand, is to clear away the misconceptions that impede an understanding of the writer's work, and to offer an interpretation that is at once free of ideology and attentive to historical reality. In these aims it is plain to me Rhoda Sirlin has succeeded admirably.

WILLIAM STYRON
MARTHA'S VINEYARD, MASSACHUSETTS
29 AUGUST 1989

Acknowledgments

I am particularly indebted to the invaluable encouragement and critical eye of the late scholar and educator Charles Child Walcutt who, having already retired from the faculty of the City University of New York Graduate School, nevertheless nurtured this project from beginning to end. His beliefs have helped to mold the theses of this book: that words in a very real sense create our reality, that artists must hold us at a distance from their subjects so that we can in fact get closer to them, and that if we go in for silence, the Holocaust will be forgotten. I am also deeply grateful to my friends Sondra Farganis and Phyllis van Slyck whose honest criticism shaped and improved this book, to my friends Lynne Deri and Sandy Lee for selfless proofreading sessions into the wee hours, and to Daniel Walden, friend and mentor, for his professional advice and assistance. To my late aunt, Helen Mofsen, who helped launch this book by retrieving and xeroxing dozens of articles from many libraries scattered throughout New York City, and to Georgette Clark, Susan Schnapf, and Cynthia Youssef, librarians at the Brooklyn Heights branch, who tirelessly tracked down often obscure material, my appreciation. Finally, many thanks to William Styron for responding graciously and frankly to my relentless questioning, and, of course, for his own considerable body of work which continues to delight and disturb his many readers.

1

Introduction

With rebellion, awareness is born. This central theme of Albert Camus' famous philosophical essay *The Rebel,* an exploration of an individual's passionate affirmation that underlies the act of rebellion, might well serve as a springboard for an understanding and appreciation of William Styron's fiction. According to Camus, the question raised by rebellion today is whether or not it is possible to find a rule of conduct outside the realm of religion and its absolute values. The rebel demands order in the midst of chaos, unity in the heart of the ephemeral. Not merely self-indulgent or resentful, then, the true rebel is concerned with communal or ethical values. By rebelling, an individual defends the dignity common to all people. Suffering saves the rebel from solitude by immersing him in a collective experience. "I rebel—therefore we exist."

The twentieth-century rebel, in particular, rebels not only against the injustice of death and the wastefulness of evil but also against a divine authority, realizing the throne of God has been overturned with human beings inheriting the crown. Without a belief in destiny, we are left mired in the throes of chance, with no divine justice. For Camus, however, the answer is not to negate everything by embracing nihilism; that is mere servitude. Real freedom is submitting to values which defy history, is learning to be human by refusing to be a god. The philosophy of the rebel is, therefore, one of limits, of a life of moderation, but a life riddled with risks.

William Styron's fiction has been and will continue to be misunderstood without an awareness of his debt to European existentialist thought, to Camus' secular humanism in particular, and without an awareness of Styron's desperate need to combat stereotypes through his fiction, stereotypes which limit the felt life. Styron's own life bears witness to this. Although Southern by birth, he is not strictly a Southern novelist. He is a transplanted Virginian who lived in Paris, founded the *Paris Review,* and then settled in Connecticut. His roots are rural and Protestant, but his fiction is primarily urban and ethnic. Styron mercilessly reveals our spiritual morass, chaos, instability, and suffering. However, he leads a rather quiet, stable life; he has been married for over three decades to an accomplished Jewish poet and Amnesty International activist, and has four children. An ex-Marine, Styron clearly mistrusts the military mind. Now a Northern liberal Democrat, Styron's Virginia Tidewater background undoubtedly shaped his humanistic values and contributed to his libertarian attacks on injustice. He has spoken eloquently against capital punishment, has helped save the life of a subliterate black man, Benjamin Reid, and has refused to write an already-paid-for article for *The New York Times Magazine* on the New York Democratic Convention because he "didn't find enough interesting material."

Styron's activities since the late 1960s reveal growing political and international concerns. In 1968, he was a delegate to the Democratic National Convention. He was a witness at the trial of the "Chicago Seven" in 1969 and was the only American writer to attend a symposium in Soviet Asia at Tashkent, the Soviet Union. In 1977 he participated in a Moscow conference of American and Soviet writers. Styron was invited to the inauguration of François Mitterrand in 1981 and that same year opposed the establishment of the Nixon Library at Duke University. In 1982 he wrote the introduction to Mitterrand's autobiography, *The Wheat and the Chaff*. Styron lobbied in Congress in 1983 on behalf of a bill which would allow authors to make tax-deductible donations of their manuscripts to nonprofit institutions. In 1984 he attended an Amnesty International conference in Tokyo. In 1988 he protested the nomination of Judge Robert Bork to the Supreme Court. Most recently he and members of the Freedom-to-Write Committee of the American Center of PEN sent a letter to the Israeli government urging it "to cease its practice of censorship" of Palestinian writers and journalists in the West Bank and Gaza. This letter, drafted after months of heated discussion, has divided some of the leading writers in the United States. He has also protested the censoring of Salman Rushdie's *The Satanic Verses*. Styron, in short, has been able to wed literary and political interests, disproving the notion that only Europeans know how to mix literature and politics.

This biographical information is crucial insofar as it helps us to understand the criticism that has been levied against his writing. His first novel, *Lie Down in Darkness* (1951), although winning for Styron at age twenty-six the Prix de Rome of the American Academy of Arts and Letters, was thought "not Southern enough" by many critics, not the new *The Sound and the Fury*; Styron suffered because he chose not to be a mere recipient of a tradition which promotes and glorifies the Southern past. He then wrote *The Long March* (1953), an anti-war novella, unfashionable in the 1950s. In the book the Marines became a symbol of American totalitarianism, but in the television production of the novella, Styron's unorthodox stand was watered down to make it more palatable for the American audience. In 1960 Styron published his second novel, *Set This House on Fire,* again a disappointment to many critics partially because it veered even further from his Southern roots. Most of the action takes place in a small Italian village populated by self-indulgent, corrupt Americans who bring crassness and violence to the Italian villagers. Here Styron rejects the stereotype of the naive American corrupted by European wickedness. His fourth novel, *The Confessions of Nat Turner* (1967), although winning a Pulitzer Prize, generated bitter attacks because it was not pro-black enough. Some thought it an outrage that a Southern white man could pretend to understand the mind of a black slave, to speak with a black man's voice, this in the middle of the fiercely political black nationalist movement of the late 1960s. Styron urges us not to lump all slaves or slaveowners into one stereotyped category. His research led him to the conclusion that black insurrections were the exception and not the rule in pre-Civil War America, again an unpopular notion in the late 1960s.

His fifth and most recent novel, *Sophie's Choice* (1979), was on the hardcover bestseller list for forty-seven weeks and won the American Book Award for fiction. Despite this acclaim, the novel offended some who thought it in poor taste to create a non-Jewish heroine who survived the Nazi concentration camps—a Christian survivor of Nazi totalitarianism. Some thought it even more audacious for Styron to fuse Jewish and Southern literary traditions, two of America's richest literary heritages. Yet Styron links what are for him the two horrors of modern times—slavery and genocide in the American South, and slavery and genocide in Nazi Eastern Europe. One of the epigraphs to *Sophie's Choice* is a line from André Malraux's *Lazare:* "I seek that essential region of the soul where absolute evil confronts brotherhood." The absolute evil that Styron dramatizes in the novel is what became known on both the slave auction blocks and in the Nazi concentration camps as "selection," the separation of families and friends into those sent off to die and those sent off to be worked to death. The Old South's "final solution" was also America's "absolute evil." Clearly, many critics will not let this parallel go unchallenged.

For Styron, if the Holocaust is the central horror of the twentieth century, it is not because it was anti-Semitic but because it was anti-life. Holding on to repressive traditions too is anti-life, as is any belief in absolute values. Styron's fiction provides no answers but urges us instead to question everything. Affirmations, then, are singular, personal; his optimism is provisional. Hope can often sap up of our needed strength to combat injustices on earth. Styron has been criticized for his supposed pessimism, yet out of despair artists create. Styron would argue that all great art has been born of a pessimistic view of life often brought out of perilous times and out of suffering. If we can overcome the need to stereotype, the need not to think, awareness is born, and with awareness comes action, and with action comes personal meaning. Here Styron echoes Camus' sentiments: in a world of unhappiness, we must create happiness.

Many of Styron's fictional characters, however, are unable to create happiness. Many seem afflicted with an acute case of emotional and intellectual arrest, stifled by Romantic and Puritan myths, unable to live in the present. Styron often uses interior monologues to portray our spiritual malaise; nostalgic reveries, however, cannot cure the illness. Some characters choose suicide, some murder, some prolong their agony by living a dead life. Many just hide behind outdated political, religious, or artistic abstractions. But for Styron and Camus, to be fully human is to doubt. One either chooses the creative present, this world, or one chooses death. Finding spiritual sustenance in our modern wasteland is the job of the living. Resisting nihilism, therefore, is one of Styron's most urgent themes. Human beings must demand meaning in a world that denies it; this is the true absurd position but, for Styron, the only liberating one. Since there is no absolute order, knowledge, or salvation, only humanistic values can combat the senselessness of violence, the purposelessness of most of our lives.

The first step towards this renewal is accepting our loss of innocence. The pervasive myth of the American Adam is stultifying, even treacherous, according to Styron. In this way, Styron is countering a dominant stream of American writers who yearn for an Edenic past, rebuking the prevailing American tendency towards nostalgia, a tendency which produces stunted individuals and often less-than-great fiction. Styron's vision, then, is closer to Melville's than to Emerson's or Whitman's. Evil is not merely the privation of good; it lies within us, not in abstract systems, for it is we who create divisive, destructive systems which serve to separate us. After visiting Auschwitz, Styron asked not where God was but where humanity was. The emergence of maturity and the ability to love require the purging of self-illusions and grandiose Puritan and Romantic myths. One must rebel to grow, and even failed rebellion is preferable to mere Faulknerian endurance. Suffering and struggle can indeed be purgative, creative; rebellion and struggle, therefore, dominate all of Styron's fiction.

Styron's work proves that the novel is still a plausible art form, that literature is still worthy of a kind of faith, one that can transform us by providing us with knowledge and order. Although Styron tampers with chronology and different points of view, he is basically a traditional novelist who worries about plot, character, and setting, and who concerns himself with the lofty themes of his literary forebears—goodness, evil, race, slavery, time, love, death, and redemption. The writers for whom he has a particular fondness are Tolstoy, Conrad, Flaubert, Melville, Faulkner, Fitzgerald, Thomas Wolfe, Walker Percy, and Philip Roth. Because Styron is a man firmly rooted in the present, he has been able to merge his literary and political passions. Yet he is no mere apologist defending or justifying particular political philosophies. His fiction urges us instead to resist propaganda, to resist stereotypes or easy solutions, to reject lies. It is not through hope but through revolt that human beings can establish justice on earth. With rebellion, awareness is born. It is this seemingly simple yet revolutionary ethic that will be explored here in Styron's fiction.

Americans have warmly embraced Camus' secular ethics, his atheistic humanism, despite our pretensions towards religious piety. Yet Camus was censured and even ostracized at home for his unorthodox truths. American writers like Poe, Hemingway, Faulkner, and Styron have found receptive audiences in Europe while meeting with criticism at home. The best American writers have always been able to give body and voice to the tragic elements that our society officially wishes to ignore but which exist in the unspoken consciousness of many. Styron has spoken out for those who keep silent, but in so doing he has run the heavy risk of being ostracized by American critics and readers.

Styron confesses at the outset of *Sophie's Choice*, through an epigraph by Rainer Maria Rilke, that the whole of death is beyond description just as the act of love is, yet he attempts to describe both in this great novel. Auschwitz, Styron says, must remain the one place on earth most unyielding to meaning or definition. Auschwitz is an ever-present reminder that our fate will be sealed the day we forget how to love. Styron's fiction reminds us just how fragile love is, that the essential "choice" we all make is between death and the love of the living. Although Styron has not lived the life of a pariah, his works have been nonetheless revolutionary. Tacked to his studio wall is a famous line from Flaubert: "Be regular and orderly in your life like a Bourgeois so that you may be violent and original in your work."

Although *Sophie's Choice* won the American Book Award for fiction, it met with some very mixed reviews. Generally favorable reviews appeared in the *Christian Science Monitor, Commonweal, The Atlantic Monthly, Time, America, The New Statesman, The New York Times Book Review, Newsweek, Commentary, The Virginia Quarterly Review, The Yale Review, The Village Voice,* and *Vogue.* Critics such as Doris Grumbach, Paul Fussell, John Gardner, Gail Godwin, Peter Prescott, Jonathan Yardley, and Larzer Ziff regard *Sophie's Choice* as at least a major work if not a masterpiece.

Some critics, however, regard the novel as bombastic and melodramatic—in short, a colossal failure. Robert Towers in *The New York Review of Books* argues that the voice of Stingo and other deficiencies make it difficult to regard the novel as even a noble failure. Robert Alter in *Saturday Review* contends that the ties between the personal frame and historical subject do not quite hold. Julian Symons in the *Times Literary Supplement* also argues that the novel is divided into two parts that are not very closely stitched together, that the novel is a melodrama and not a tragedy. John Aldridge in *Harper's* asserts that the novel has no ideas to express, that Styron uses pyrotechnics. Jack Beatty in *The New Republic* calls the novel sluggish, self-indulgent, dull, wordy, and windy. *The New Yorker* calls the novel contrived, humorless, overwrought, and ponderous. And David Evanier in *National Review* calls *Sophie's Choice* not a novel but copious notes towards a novel, totally lacking in form, the bad writing of which is more memorable than the good.

For these and other reasons, *Sophie's Choice* has engendered almost as much controversy as *The Confessions of Nat Turner* did in 1967. This book will demonstrate, however, that *Sophie's Choice* is Styron's most audacious, original, and artistically successful novel to date. First, this book will counter the many critics who have assailed the novel as anti-Semitic; *Sophie's Choice* does dramatize the madness of anti-Semitism without itself being anti-Semitic. In response to these critics who conclude that the novel tramples on sacred ground by fictionalizing the Holocaust, especially since Styron is neither a Jew nor a Holocaust survivor, this book will argue against silence in the face of the horror of the Holocaust. Fictionalizing this catastrophe does not necessarily trivialize the tragedy. A novel can, in fact, penetrate our consciousness more deeply than a historical account by affording some artistic distance—which diminishes the tendency towards numbing produced by a historical or strictly autobiographical account. Rather than trivializing the Holocaust, *Sophie's Choice* dramatizes the tragic dimensions of this unparalleled event and shows how the tragedy continues to manifest itself more than two generations after the fact, causing great anguish to its survivors and nonsurvivors, to their children and grandchildren, to Jews and Gentiles, to Europeans and Americans.

This book will also counter the argument that *Sophie's Choice* is a sexist novel, that Styron and his youthful alter ego, Stingo, are misogynists. It is true that *Sophie's Choice* explores the evils of sexism, but it is not sexist itself. Styron sets his novel in the "frozen sexual moonscape of the 1940s," a time following the Second World War of great sexual and moral confusion. Sex becomes the symbolic setting for the novel, "a nightmarish Sargasso Sea of guilts and apprehension." *Sophie's Choice* does dramatize the consequences of patriarchal cultures which make men and women victims and victimizers, that force us to behave according to stereotyped roles. For this Styron has been branded a sexist, when actually he is just demonstrating the disastrous effects of sexism on both sexes.

Finally, this book will explore the novel's powerful theme—absolute evil. The metaphor for this evil is Sophie's forced choice: she must choose which one of her two children to have murdered by the Nazis. Styron insists that evil is mysterious and inextinguishable, that Americans are not chosen people exempt from the world's demonism; American innocence is shown as potentially lethal. *Sophie's Choice* is then an American spiritual journey into the mystery of iniquity, a twentieth-century *Moby-Dick*. The many Melvillean overtones will be explored, linking Styron to the great nineteenth-century anti-Transcendental novelists such as Hawthorne, Melville, Twain, and James, a noble tradition which continues in twentieth-century writers like Faulkner and Styron who have a tragic view of the human condition. While insisting on the power and inextinguishability of evil in human beings and nature, Styron ultimately provides a compassionate vision of humanity struggling for meaning in an indifferent universe. The characters in *Sophie's Choice,* although limited by heredity and environment, are still capable of great love and loyalty despite their suffering, despite the obvious madness of the twentieth century. In this sense, although the evil that is the Holocaust pervades this novel, so too does brotherhood, and that is why the novel's epigraph, "I seek that essential region of the soul where absolute evil confronts brotherhood," is not only apposite to the theme but also reveals Styron's daring as a novelist—his ability to give voice to a few of the "beaten and butchered and betrayed and martyred children of the earth." In a world which permitted the black edifice of Auschwitz, *Sophie's Choice* asserts, albeit tentatively, that love may yet be possible, that loving must not be an absurdity after Auschwitz. *Sophie's Choice* urges us to conquer our grief through love and laughter, without which aggression against the self or others is the only alternative.

In an era of fashionable postmodern minimalism and nihilism, Styron has created characters who seek the high-minded solace that is available in self-knowledge, in the future, in love. Styron is one of the few contemporary novelists who create characters still struggling for transcendence, showing that life is serious, not just trivial and grim, that characters can make important though limited choices, that there are issues worth clarifying. By insisting on affirming the values the Nazis denied their victims, Styron makes the human face richer and more admirable.

Styron, therefore, must be appreciated as one of the most audacious and humane voices in contemporary literature. With tremendous sympathy for the casualties of history, he continues to be on the side of the humiliated, the persecuted, and the suffering. While all of his fiction has been concerned with human domination and with the pathos of victims of that domination, *Sophie's Choice* in particular dramatizes the horrific consequences of a victimizer's inability to identify with his victim. *Sophie's Choice* dares to try to understand and express compassion for victims and victimizers. It is to be hoped that Styron will continue to challenge the moral and intellectual complacency of his readers with fiction that demonstrates that there is no rational order in existence, that human beings are at risk of extinction, and that rebellion, therefore, in a post-Holocaust world is critical to our survival as a species.

2

Against Sacred Silences:
Holocaust Fiction and Anti-Semitism

Elie Wiesel, Nobel Peace Prize recipient for 1986, dedicated his award to the survivors of the Nazis for teaching "humankind how not to succumb to despair" (Joseph Berger). Wiesel has emerged as an important spiritual leader, seeing the need to help all the living who suffer—whether victims of oppression in Cambodia and South Africa or Soviet Jews forbidden to emigrate—in short, victims of violence, repression, and racism. As a survivor of the Nazi concentration camps himself, Wiesel is obsessed with his own need to bear witness to the Holocaust in deference to all those who died in the camps, to make sure none of us ever forgets.

It is all the more paradoxical, then, that Wiesel also claims that writing cannot change attitudes, that it is futile to try to explain or imagine the unimaginable. Between the dead and the rest of us, he claims, there exists an abyss that no talent can comprehend. Wiesel is caught in a conflict between the need to recount and the realization that all explanation is futile. For him Auschwitz is sacred, transcending all language. A nonsurvivor can only trivialize the Holocaust; so those capable of sincerity and humility will withdraw without entering into the heart of the matter. Particularly upsetting to him is any attempt to portray the executioners as human beings or to try to make us understand them. To universalize the Holocaust is to trivialize it. If Auschwitz is beyond vocabulary, Wiesel can urge only sacred silence. Auschwitz, Wiesel contends, in a recent *New York Times* article,

> defeated art, because just as no one could imagine Auschwitz before Auschwitz, no one can retell Auschwitz after Auschwitz. The truth of Auschwitz remains hidden in its ashes. Only those who lived it in their flesh and in their minds can possibly transform their experience into knowledge. Others, despite their best intentions, can never do so. (1)

Literature and art can never succeed in communicating the final reality of the human condition during the Holocaust. For Wiesel, the only way, then, to keep the memory of all those slaughtered by the Nazis alive is to study the texts,

> such as the diaries of Emanuel Ringelblum and Chaim Kaplan; the works by the historians Raul Hilberg, Lucy Davidowicz, Martin Gilbert, Michael Marrus. Watch the documentaries—such as Alain Resnais's "Night and Fog," Claude Lanzmann's "Shoah" and Haim Gouri's "81st Blow." Listen to the survivors and respect their wounded sensibility. Open yourselves to their scarred memory, and mingle your tears with theirs. And stop insulting the dead. (38)

In this same article in *The New York Times* called "Art and the Holocaust: Trivializing Memory," Wiesel singles out Styron (whom he calls simply "an American novelist") as the one who recently suggested that the suicide of novelist and Holocaust survivor Primo Levi was "nothing but a bout of depression that good psychoanalytical treatment could have cured" (38). Wiesel feels that Styron has reduced Primo Levi to a banal nervous breakdown, thereby trivializing the tragedy of a great writer, "a man who never ceased to battle the black angel of Auschwitz" (38).

If we look at what Styron said about Primo Levi in an article which appeared in *The New York Times* on 19 December 1988, we discover that he felt Mr. Levi's death "could not be dissociated from the major depression with which he was afflicted, and that indeed his suicide proceeded directly from that illness" ("Why Primo Levi Need Not Have Died," A17). Styron further explains, however, that "Mr. Levi may have been bedeviled by buried conflicts unrelated to Auschwitz. Or, indeed, his ordeal at Auschwitz may have imposed on his soul an insupportable burden" (A17). Obviously, Wiesel has distorted Styron's position, for clearly Styron is well aware that many writers wounded by the Holocaust have decided upon suicide to eradicate painful memories eternally; indeed, his fictional Holocaust survivor, Sophie Zawistowska, found her ordeal at Auschwitz so insupportable a burden that she chose to swallow a cyanide tablet. Styron is not offering simplistic psychological bromides to explain the behavior of Holocaust survivors; he is merely asserting that suicidal depression, whatever the cause, is a malignant disease, that some people suffering from this disease can be helped with proper treatment, and that no moral blame should be placed on those who choose suicide.

Wiesel muses, "Such, then, is the victory of the executioner: by raising his crimes to a level beyond the imagining and understanding of men, he planned to deprive his victims of any hope of sharing their monstrous meaning with others" (1). An artistic rendering of this monstrous victimization which has sufficient imagination, sincerity, skill, and fidelity to historical truth can give voice and hope to Holocaust survivors, thereby diminishing the victory of the executioner, who must not, after all, have the last word. The unuttered cry must not be the loudest; that way lies total victory for the victimizer. A great artist is compelled to understand and give voice to both victim and victimizer.

Wiesel is not the only prominent cultural figure to urge silence. Bruno Bettelheim, a concentration-camp victim and noted psychologist, also argues against universalizing the Holocaust. He recently reviewed Dr. Robert Jay Lifton's *The Nazi Doctors,* asserting that the effort to understand the vile Nazi doctors is itself wrong "because of the ever-present danger that understanding fully may come close to forgiving" ("Their Specialty Was Murder" 62). Lifton responded that he "wrote a book on Nazi doctors to combat evil with knowledge of evil behavior" (56). Lifton's previous book, *Death in Life: Survivors of Hiroshima,* is a sympathetic study of what psychiatrists now call post-traumatic syndrome and survivor guilt. Bettelheim, describing his experiences in the concentration camps at Dachau and Buchenwald in *The Informed Heart,* writes, "Heart and reason can no longer be kept in their separate places. . . . Our hearts must know the world of reason, and reason must be guided by an informed heart" (viii). It seems that Bettelheim, like Wiesel, feels a conflict between the need to recount and the fear that understanding the Nazis comes close to forgiving them.

The German theorist Theodor Adorno, a prominent member of the Frankfurt School of critical thought, also contends that there are no words to describe the unimaginable. There is, he feels, no possibility for poetry after Auschwitz.

Similarly, George Steiner, literary critic and cultural historian, has written passionately on the subject of language and literature in this post-Holocaust era. His two books, *In Bluebeard's Castle: Some Notes towards the Redefinition of Culture* and *Language and Silence: Essays on Language, Literature and the Inhuman,* explore the possibility of language approximating the horror of the Holocaust. In his essay "Silence and the Poet," Steiner states that the word must fail in the face of the inhuman. He therefore suggests silence: "Nothing speaks louder than the unwritten poem" (54). The world of Auschwitz, he asserts, lies outside of speech as it lies outside of reason.

Professor Alvin H. Rosenfeld, author of *A Double Dying: Reflections on Holocaust Literature* and *Imagining Hitler,* is particularly critical of fictionalizing the Holocaust. The Holocaust is reduced, he argues, in the realm of fiction. At a Modern Language Association Convention panel discussion in 1986 entitled "Imagining the Unimaginable: American Literature and the Holocaust," Rosenfeld declared that we are in danger of "losing the Holocaust through metaphor." He chastised William Styron for misappropriating Auschwitz, reducing the war against the Jews to sexual combat. *Sophie's Choice,* for him, is a spoof of the Holocaust which exploits this atrocity and should be more appropriately entitled "The Erotics of Auschwitz." Rosenfeld further declared that Stingo, the narrator of *Sophie's Choice*, is more interested in recreating Sophie than understanding the Holocaust and, in the process, mocks the authenticity of Sophie's anguish. Stingo, and Styron by extension, therefore, are seen as pathetic egotists.

Lawrence Langer, author of *Versions of Survival: The Holocaust and the Human Spirit* and *The Holocaust and the Literary Imagination*, argues that artists must struggle to invent images equal to the horror of historical events. Works of literature, he claims, make atrocity accessible to the imagination even as the ordeal of atrocity slips from human memory and drives us to reconsider how its ravages affect love and hope in the modern world. Yet in a paper delivered at the 1986 MLA Convention, entitled "The Holocaust as Background and Foreground in *Sophie's Choice* and *Mr. Sammler's Planet*," Langer praised Saul Bellow for remaining silent on Mr. Sammler's days spent in a concentration camp and criticized William Styron for trespassing on sacred terrain.

Morris Dickstein, author of a book on the culture of the 1960s entitled *Gates of Eden*, thinks Styron's novel is less about the Holocaust than about William Styron himself. Dickstein believes that many modern writers shy away from social and political phenomena and write only about themselves. *Sophie's Choice*, for him, is merely "technicolor melodramatics" (391). A critic upset that too much fiction is concerned with the self as subject, that too much fiction is unconnected with the real world, he also argues that silence would be the more appropriate response to the Holocaust.

An even more extreme view comes from Irving Saposnik, lecturer in English at the University of Haifa in Israel. Saposnik argues that Styron creates Jewish fictional characters and chooses to write about the Holocaust so that he can be in the company of the Holy Trinity of Jewish American writers—Bellow, Malamud, and Roth. On the one hand, he argues that Nathan Landau is Styron's most compelling and tragic Jewish character, while also asserting that Nathan's self-destructiveness is symbolic of Styron's "goyish revenge—the attack of the Southern boy on the urban Jewish mafia" (332).

Alan L. Berger, author of *Crisis and Covenant: The Holocaust in American Jewish Fiction*, argues that

> *Sophie's Choice* fails to comprehend the Jewish specificity of the Holocaust. Ahistorical in method, Styron's novel deals not so much with an epoch-making event, but with human existence in extremity, sexuality, slavery, and stereotype. This kind of Holocaust novel encourages trivialization by ignoring the interconnection between the destiny of Judaism and the fate of Western civilization. . . . *Sophie's Choice*, while capitalizing on

the Holocaust fad, if one may use that term, raises a serious problem. It may well be the case that Styron accomplishes in the literary world what the so-called revisionists—the falsifiers and deniers of history—are trying to achieve using academics and the gullible public, de-Judaizing the Holocaust. (33)

Cynthia Ozick, acclaimed fiction writer and essayist, criticizes Styron's approach to the Holocaust in an article entitled "A Liberal's Auschwitz" which appeared in *The Pushcart Prize: Best of the Small Presses* in 1976. In 1974 after visiting Auschwitz, Styron wrote an article which appeared on *The New York Times* Op-Ed page in which he observed that Auschwitz was not only anti-Jewish but "anti-human. Anti-life." Ozick argues that this liberal view of Auschwitz is too egalitarian; it levels too much. She says, "If we make an abstraction out of human wickedness—as when Mr. Styron wants to call the Auschwitz impulse 'anti-human' and 'anti-life' rather than 'narrowly' anti-Semitic—we will soon forget that every wickedness has had a habitation and a name" (152). Ozick contends that Styron uses the Jews as mere metaphors by insisting on the "ecumenical nature" of the tragedy, that he has sought to lessen his and our pain by blurring issues, by shunning specificity.

There are two arguments, then, against Styron's having written a book exploring the Holocaust. The lesser of the two arguments is that Styron is not a survivor himself and is not Jewish, that he does not fully appreciate the Holocaust as a Jewish phenomenon, that he somehow trespassed on property not rightfully his. The larger, more philosophical issue involved is that nobody, Jew or Gentile, should fictionalize the Holocaust, that the proper response is to be silent in the face of this horror lest one trivialize or universalize it. Dealing with the Holocaust is seen as dignifying it. Literature, in this view, can merely bear witness to the pain; it cannot help transcend the pain.

But there is a strong opposing point of view, a view which many, including Styron, support. Many argue that the power of the imagination to evoke an atmosphere does far more than historians' fidelity to facts. In this view, nonliterary accounts of life in the concentration camps could numb the consciousness because of the enormity of the atrocities. One, then, does not lose the Holocaust through metaphor or trivialize it; indeed, it is history that is inadequate. Literature has the potential to contribute more than history or philosophy to our ethical and public lives.

Much recent fiction, however, has been termed minimalist and narcissistic; that is, fiction focusing on inner journeys that lead nowhere, neither to a fuller understanding of history as refracted through a single life nor even to a fuller understanding of the self. In Christopher Lasch's recent book, *The Minimal Self: Psychic Survival in Troubled Times,* he argues that today's artists cannot even understand history, let alone change it, unlike early twentieth-century artists who "humanized the industrial order, and chastened the spirit of materialism and acquisitiveness" (162). Even Philip Roth feels that fiction can no longer compete with today's headlines. But can this charge fairly be levied against Styron? *Sophie's Choice* is neither minimalist nor narcissistic. Stingo's inner journey does lead somewhere—to a fuller understanding of history as refracted through Sophie and to a fuller understanding of the self, the all-too-innocent American self.

Perhaps the best response to the charge that since Styron is not Jewish he had no right to appropriate the Holocaust comes from Allan A. Ryan, Jr., one-time director of the Justice Department's Office of Special Investigation for Nazi war crimes and one of the foremost Nazi hunters in this country. When a reporter asked him how he got involved with Nazi hunting, Ryan responded:

> How can a Ryan not get into it? I've never seen this as a Jewish issue. It should concern everybody. It happened to all of us. But we're not here to avenge the Holocaust. We're here to apply the law. (Blumenthal)

When asked what he learned from his involvement, he stated:

> I understand I understand so little. I do not understand how people could have done this. How could people have done this to each other? How could it have happened? I have to say, at last, I don't understand. (Blumenthal)

While no one can avenge the Holocaust, Ryan has found a way to fight back and so has Styron. Stingo is forced to learn how to conquer grief and despair, and, by extension, so must we all.

What about Bruno Bettelheim's argument that to understand the Nazis comes perilously close to forgiving them? Other psychologists and psychiatrists are diametrically opposed to Bettelheim's assumption. Dr. Robert Jay Lifton, as previously mentioned, is a psychiatrist dedicated to understanding evil behavior in order to combat it. His books examining the victims of the camps, Hiroshima, and Nazi doctors bear this out. Another psychiatrist known for his work on understanding human evil is Dr. M. Scott Peck, author of *People of the Lie: The Hope for Healing Human Evil*. The basic premise of his book is that we cannot heal what we do not even dare study, maintaining that evil is inherently and inevitably mysterious. He agrees with Hannah Arendt's description of evil: that it is basically banal, ordinary, common. Evil, for Peck, is an illness, an object for research. Those who are evil are those who oppose the life force, who, in his view, deserve more pity than hatred. Evil originates not in the absence of guilt but in the effort to escape it. We cannot conquer evil by destroying it; evil can be conquered only through love. *Sophie's Choice* is a dramatic representation of this basic philosophical viewpoint.

Alice Miller is another influential psychoanalyst who has written three books in the 1980s exploring the roots of evil, violence, and madness: *The Drama of the Gifted Child; For Your Own Good: Hidden Cruelty in Child-Rearing and the Roots of Violence;* and *Thou Shalt Not Be Aware: Society's Betrayal of the Child.* Her books are considered so seditious that she had to leave her native Germany and write, publish, and practice in Switzerland. What makes her work radical is that she believes human destructiveness is a reactive (not innate) phenomenon, that every persecutor was once a victim; thus, the need to commit murder is the outcome of a tragic childhood. "Those children who are beaten will beat, those intimidated will intimidate, those humiliated will humiliate and those whose souls are murdered will murder" (232). Miller indicts any society which rears its children through physical force or humiliation and which claims it is for their own good. She sees much of Western family life as prototypical of a totalitarian regime in which the highest good is obedience and the weaker are humiliated (women and children). Included in her book *For Your Own Good* is a frightening chapter on Hitler's childhood which describes the daily beatings he received from his father starting at two years old and continuing throughout his childhood while his mother watched submissively. It is precisely this Prussian family structure which produces a totalitarian state. Her most urgent and enduring message is that we aid and abet inhuman behavior by our innocence and naivete. Here, Styron would most fervently agree.

When Styron wrote *Sophie's Choice,* he was familiar with the works of Wiesel, Bettelheim, Steiner, and Arendt, with autobiographical accounts of those victimized in the concentration camps, and with Rudolf Höss's autobiographical *The Commandant of Auschwitz.* Some of the novel was influenced, then, by outside reading—reading which informs the voice of the older, reflective narrator. Part-way through the book Styron felt the need to visit Auschwitz personally, impelled by the memory of a Catholic Polish girl who became Sophie. What he learned on this visit was that "Auschwitz must remain the one place on earth most unyielding to meaning or definition" (*This Quiet Dust and Other Writings* 303).

The bulk of the novel, however, is more imaginatively felt than researched. Here it would be appropriate to explore Styron's ideas on the art and purpose of fiction and then his specific feelings about his use of the Holocaust in his fiction. All of Styron's writing (fiction and nonfiction) reveals a sense of engagement and commitment to public life like that of Camus, Sartre, and Malraux, whose writings have clearly influenced him. Camus' 1957 definition of the role of writers, which appeared in *Resistance, Rebellion, and Death,* parallels Styron's approach:

The artist of today becomes unreal if he remains in his ivory tower or sterilized if he spends his time galloping around the political arena. Yet between the two lies the arduous way of true art. It seems to me that the writer must be fully aware of the dramas of his time and that he must take sides every time he can or knows how to do so. (238)

Styron believes that literature can and must change us by penetrating our consciousness. History is inadequate to do this. Literature does more than inform; it can help raise our consciousness of horror and pain, can change future behavior. Art, then, according to Styron, has the right to break in upon even sacred silence, a view most at odds with Steiner and Wiesel.

While literature has the potential to raise consciousness, it is unlikely that mass media could have that potential. Styron feels that television generally fears the truth, which can only poison art. In this regard, then, the subject of the Holocaust is beyond the capacities of mass media. Certainly Styron is not an authority on Auschwitz or the Holocaust, nor does he claim to be. He has another vision, another metaphor, which enables us to feel the Holocaust, which for Styron is awesomely central to our present-day consciousness—in fact, is the central issue of the twentieth century. The metaphor for absolute evil Styron chose was a woman's having to decide which of her children was to be murdered. Styron understands that the Holocaust must be more than an image or symbol of modern malaise; it must serve as a warning or incentive to social action. Cynicism and nihilism are not answers. We must be able to imagine a moral order that transcends this unparalleled horror.

In this regard, *Sophie's Choice* is not so much a story about Auschwitz but of discovering evil, a story which unfolds through uniquely American eyes—Stingo's eyes. *Sophie's Choice* is Stingo's tale and as such is a *Bildungsroman*. The education is in pain, in vicarious and literal suffering. By the end of the novel, Stingo is no longer a stranger to love and death, to suffering, evil, and madness. If the novel, then, is more about discovering evil than about Auschwitz per se, Styron manages to gain some distance this way. He is able to transcend the fidelity to facts, which is the historian's domain, and concentrate instead on psychological or poetic truths. Dates and statistics are less important than imagination. It is true that Styron's fiction contains a portrait of the real-life Commandant of Auschwitz, Rudolf Höss, but this portrait is more imaginatively felt since very little is actually known about his private life or inner motivations. Styron justifies his inclusion of the Commandant in his fiction on these grounds, whereas he would never have included, say, a portrait of Himmler because too much is actually known about him. The same is true for his fictional portrait of Nat Turner, about whom little is known.

What Styron wants to portray in his novel is the ecumenical nature of the evil of Nazi totalitarianism. While the Holocaust is an unparalleled tragedy for the Jews, it is actually a threat to all humanity. The novel's purpose was not to erect a monument to the suffering of the Jews, although Styron's pain is clearly evident in the writing, and his portrayal of European and American anti-Semitism is unflinching. The novel deals with the oppressors and the victims in an effort to demonstrate that absolute evil has never and will never vanish from the world, that the dominant theme in history has been the propensity for human beings to dominate one another. Hannah Arendt said about the Holocaust that once a crime has appeared for the first time, its reappearance is more likely. Styron, like his European literary forebears Camus, Sartre, and Malraux, has been able to wed literature and politics, the public and the private, and history and the novel.

Because *Sophie's Choice* was on the hardcover bestseller list for forty-seven weeks and won the American Book Award for fiction in May 1980, naturally Styron was given much media attention, particularly lengthy interviews in which he answered questions about the themes in his work, his habits, the process of creation, and especially about why he chose to write about the Holocaust. It would be instructive here to include some of Styron's responses to critics shortly after the publication of *Sophie's Choice* and to record, ironically, his conviction that Jews would not object to his novel. First, when asked if he had a central theme or subject, Styron responded:

> I suppose the pathos of the victim has always been a central consideration in what I've written—the victimization of people by life or by other human beings, sometimes even to the extent that it has to do, at its most extreme, with slavery. That's always seemed to me to be a very important artistic theme—what other people do to each other in the guise of idealism or of passion or of zealotry, whatever. (West 234–35)

When asked whether life in the concentration camps figures largely in the novel or rather its aftereffects, with the characters looking back on their lives, Styron answered:

> I felt in this theme that it would be presumptuousness of a large order to try to re-create life in a concentration camp in any way. I'm simply not going to do that. We all know the bare outlines of this thing. But it's too horrible to even contemplate. So, what I've already done is merely to suggest the horror of the place by recording in an almost documentary way certain points, some of the recorded statements made by the victims, and some of the statements and diaries of the SS men that ran the camp, doing this simply to suggest the horror, because you can't really do justice to the horror by attempting to say that one's fictional character did such and such a thing and was victimized to this extent on such and such a day because, as I say, it would be almost sacrilegious to intrude on that kind of extreme experience. (West 197–98)

Another interviewer asked Styron how he was able to write about Auschwitz despite his going into a state of complete emotional shock after having seen the barbed wires, fences, barracks, and human remains first-hand. Styron responded:

> Perhaps because of the Malraux sentence which I used as an epigraph. It was my friend Carlos Fuentes who called my attention to this sentence from *Lazare:* "I seek that essential region of the soul where absolute evil confronts brotherhood." It seemed to me that if I could reach this area, this moment, I could try—as much as was in my power—to elucidate one of the major mysteries of the history of twentieth-century man. It seemed that if I could develop a metaphor to represent this "confrontation," if I could recreate this moment of absolute evil under some form plausible to the reader, taking my own capabilities and the imperfections of art into account, then I would be taking up Malraux's challenge; I would be doing what every writer must try to do. (West 253–54)

In a more recent interview, in 1983, after the novel had already provoked a good deal of controversy, Styron was asked whether he was worried when he wrote the novel about the view that only survivors should attempt to recreate the Holocaust in literature or film and whether any attempt to recreate it necessarily diminished the event. In typically direct fashion, Styron asserted:

> No. Of course, I was perfectly aware of the argument in favor of silence, and also the argument that says that anyone who is not a survivor is incapable of rendering the story. I simply don't agree with either of those points of view. I realized I was treading on very delicate ground, and I did not want to rush into it in any haphazard way. I knew there was a risk, but at the same time I balked at the idea that, as horrible as it was, the Holocaust was some sort of sacrosanct area that could not be treated. I especially balked at the idea that someone who was not there was incapable of dealing with it. If that is true, then it is true for all experience. It would have prevented our greatest Civil War novel from having been written. *The Red Badge of Courage* was written by Stephen Crane, a man who was never within a hundred miles of a battlefield, and yet it remains our most powerful document about the combat side of civil war. (West 257)

The interviewer then remarked that Elie Wiesel and his colleagues would presumably argue that the enormity of the Holocaust was qualitatively different. Against it, even evocations of the Civil War are diminished. Styron answered:

> I certainly understand that aspect of the argument. And for that reason, I approached the subject with as much humility as I could muster. I realized that I was dealing with something totally unusual, not an ordinary catastrophe, but an exceptional catastrophe of universal scope. Even so, I could not be persuaded that this should prevent someone from dealing with it. (West 257–58)

Styron was equally direct about his confidence in the reception of his novel by Jewish readers while acknowledging some fear that his novel would be misconstrued. In 1980 he said:

> I was, to be honest, somewhat worried that it would be misconstrued by the Jewish readers but I found, to my pleasant surprise, that it wasn't. I thought there might be some objections to a goy attacking the question of the Holocaust and to the notion that for almost the first time you had a major character in a literary work who was not Jewish and who was a victim of the Nazis, which of course is true of Sophie. She's not a Jew, she went to Auschwitz, and she is a victim. I had to say to myself from time to time that this is not the pattern, that Jews were the major victims, but I also had to face the fact that there were other victims and I was determined to put that down. I think it's a great tribute to the honoring of truth by Jews in general that there has been no objection to this. (West 235)

This, unfortunately, did not prove to be true, but might have seemed so shortly after the publication of *Sophie's Choice,* perhaps because Styron had been so viciously attacked and called a racist, particularly by blacks, in the late 1960s after the *The Confessions of Nat Turner.* In the last few years, Styron has been called anti-Semitic, and *Sophie's Choice* is read as anti-Semitic by some Jewish readers on two grounds: first, that Sophie is a Polish Catholic survivor of Auschwitz and should have been Jewish; and second, that the one major Jewish character in the novel, Nathan Landau, is sadistic and insane, which supposedly reflects the deep anti-Semitic feelings of many Gentiles, notably, William Styron himself. Both of these arguments can be refuted by other readers and Styron himself, but it is sad that a novel which explores the insanity of anti-Semitism should be attacked as anti-Semitic itself. When this writer asked Styron whether he was upset that some were calling his novel anti-Semitic, Styron first looked pained, and then replied, "Nothing could be as bad as the response to *Nat Turner.*" Underneath that observation was sadness and dismay at having been so misunderstood again. Had Styron attended the panel on Holocaust writing at the Modern Language Association Convention in New York in 1986, he would have witnessed a tremendous amount of venom directed against him for creating a non-Jewish victim of the Holocaust and for creating a demonic Jewish character compelled to batter a non-Jewish survivor.

Before countering those who claim that *Sophie's Choice* is anti-Semitic, it would be instructive to trace American public awareness of the Holocaust, a general awareness which is surprisingly recent. Like Stingo right after the Second World War, Americans were as a rule quite ignorant and naive about the concentration camps. It is only in the last few years that scholars are openly documenting and criticizing the lack of American Jewish unity and organization during the war years and President Roosevelt's decision not to bomb the camps even though their locations were well known by the military, all of which is presented in David S. Wyman's book, *The Abandonment of the Jews,* published in 1984. In general, the public knew little about the Holocaust in the late 1940s and 1950s, a time of peace, prosperity, and comfort at home, a time when not much literature had been published on the subject.

American consciousness, however, began to rise in the early 1960s with the capture of Adolf Eichmann in South America and his subsequent televised trial in Jerusalem in April of 1961. Americans watched and listened to "the man in the glass booth" who claimed he was totally loyal to the laws of his land, that killing Jews was not murder but mercy killing. Americans learned that the Nazis destroyed much evidence before the end of the war because they knew that mass murder, because of its novelty, would not be accepted by other nations. In 1963 Hannah Arendt published her groundbreaking book *Eichmann in Jerusalem: A Report on the Banality of Evil,* which further educated the public. Arendt's still-controversial thesis is that evil is banal, trite, commonplace, ordinary, and lacking in individuality, that Eichmann was not a monster, but terribly and terrifyingly normal. Eichmann was the ultimate organization man, desiring nothing more than rising in the ranks of the military bureaucracy to become part of history. Rather than being horrific, Eichmann was an obedient, law-abiding bureaucrat. What Arendt demonstrated was that a new type of criminal has been born—those who commit crimes under circumstances that make it impossible for them to know or to feel that they are doing wrong. In order to commit genocide, according to Arendt, the Nazis had to turn around their natural instincts of pity; they focused not on what horrible things they did to people but on what horrible things they had to watch in the pursuance of their duties.

By the 1970s the interest in the Nazis, the camps, and the Holocaust in general reached a peak. In the late 1970s the television program *Holocaust* was aired. While melodramatic and sensational, it nevertheless reached a wide audience, stirring public consciousness. Shortly after this program, Styron published *Sophie's Choice,* and he explains the popularity of his novel in 1979 as reflecting the spirit of the time, as coinciding with a particular *Zeitgeist.*

When Stingo first encounters Sophie, however, shortly after the war, he is totally ignorant of the enormity of Nazi crimes, of Sophie's suffering, a stranger, he says, to love and death. His limitations were the limitations of most Americans at that time. So much so, that when Stingo first saw the numbers tatooed on Sophie's arms, he assumed she must be Jewish, for only Jews suffered in the concentration camps; he was, therefore, shocked to learn that Sophie was not only not Jewish, but she was Polish and Catholic.

We can understand his surprise, but it is harder today to understand those who are shocked and angered by Sophie's being a Gentile survivor of the camps, as if Styron's creation were a perverse distortion of reality, a cruel joke. Forty years after the Second World War we know that the Jews were the chief victims of the Nazi era but not the only victims, that all those opposed to Nazi ideology were considered expendable, including, among others, the physically and mentally handicapped, homosexuals, Poles, Gypsies, and Slavs. To create a non-Jewish survivor of the Holocaust is not an anti-Semitic or insensitive act but an accurate portrait of historical realities.

When asked whether there were many non-Jews in concentration camps, Styron replied:

> About one million at Auschwitz out of four. The statistics are blurred, but if you are talking about non-Jews who died in exactly the same way as Jews, in the gas chambers, two and one half million Jews and about one million non-Jews. All this is on the historical record. Oddly enough, this is information that does not seem to bubble to the surface. It's not in the public mind. (West 232)

That response preceded the publication of the novel. Right after the publication, Styron told another reporter:

> Sophie's not a Jew, she went to Auschwitz, and she is a victim. I had to say to myself from time to time that this is not the pattern, that Jews were the major victims, but I also had to face the fact that there were other victims and I was determined to put that down. (West 235)

He further explained to another interviewer:

> With my book I would like to make people see that though the Jews were by far the principal victims of the Holocaust, there were others: the Armenians, the Gypsies, also the Poles. To ignore the existence of these victims—even if it is certain that the Jews suffered more than the others—is to minimize the Nazi horror. It is to underestimate dangerously its totalitarian dimension. (West 248)

In a more recent interview, Styron summed up his feelings on this subject:

> Part of the message, if there is such a thing as a message, in *Sophie's Choice* was that the Nazis actually got everyone. They got Jews first and foremost and most specifically, but anything so deadly, anything so utterly consummately filled with evil has to have at least a residual effect on everyone else. This seems to me the chief weakness of the totally proprietary notion of the Holocaust by Jews. Just the magnitude of the venture had to cause suffering that was universal. (West 264)

After Styron's trip to Auschwitz, and after reading a series of depositions and confessions by various SS officers who had served at Auschwitz, he realized that it would be essential to his story to make Sophie have a relationship with the Commandant. The reason for this involvement is complex and is explained by Styron this way:

> I realized that in order to make Sophie really complicated and give her other dimensions, I couldn't make her just a victim. That was very essential to the dynamism of the story. If she was just a pathetic victim she wouldn't be very interesting; but to put her in juxtaposition with the commandant—not really as a collaborator by any means but as a person who in desperation is acting in an unconventional way vis-a-vis the Nazis, trying to masquerade as a collaborator—this would give her a larger dimension. (West 237)

There are those who argue in this context that her involvement with Höss reveals her anti-Semitism. Styron feels that her character is not anti-Semitic:

> She does not hate them, at least in the beginning, and I really don't believe the character to be anti-Semitic. She must sometimes play that role because she works in the house of Höss, the commander at Auschwitz. I know, role-playing and truth, that's ambiguous. (West 247)

In short, the real Sophie was a Polish Catholic survivor, but to illuminate the totalitarian dimension of the Holocaust, Styron was compelled anyhow to make Sophie a Christian. As a Jew she would have been but one more victim, and there would not have been a novel. By using a Christian trying to masquerade as a Nazi collaborator for survival, who is a daughter of a rabid anti-Semite, Styron not only succeeded in creating a multidimensional character but also painted a portrait of the anti-Semitism of her environment, of her father, and, to be sure, of Poland at that time. A testament of that portrait is Poland's banning of Styron's novel because, obviously, it bears down so hard on Polish anti-Semitism. Sophie must struggle against the prejudices of her environment just as Stingo must struggle against the limitations of American innocence. They struggle together in Brooklyn, two Gentiles transplanted in the Kingdom of the Jews, against a history of anti-Semitism, united in their love for the dazzling but demonic Nathan Landau, Jewish con man and prophet.

This brings us to the second charge of anti-Semitism—the character of Nathan Landau and his relationship to Sophie. Looking at his name etymologically and symbolically reveals the many contradictions that make up Nathan's character. Nathan is derived from the Hebrew and means gift. Nathan was also an Old Testament prophet who rebuked King David for the death of Uriah, Bathsheba's husband, and denounced David for marrying Bathsheba after her husband's death. It was also Nathan's advice that saved the kingdom for Solomon, David's son. Perhaps, too, the name Nathan recalls Styron's other rebellious zealot, Nat Turner. The name Landau has a curious history as well. Landau is a town in Germany known for its four-wheeled covered carriages and later for a style of automobile. Landau is also the name of a Russian Jewish physicist who won the Nobel Prize for physics in 1962, accused though not convicted of spying for the Germans under Stalin's regime.

Nathan is indeed a gift, a gift to Sophie, having literally picked her off Brooklyn College library's floor, nurturing her disease-ridden, starved body back to health. Nathan also brings the gift of friendship to Stingo, a lonely Southerner among urban New Yorkers, and gives him two-hundred dollars after Stingo has been robbed, repayable only if he becomes a successful published author. Nathan's *joie de vivre* brings joy and spontaneity into the lives of Sophie and Stingo. Stingo's deepest feelings of grief and despair are caused by the deaths of his two closest friends—Nathan and Sophie. It is important to see Nathan in all his complexities and not just as Sophie's batterer. Nathan Landau resembles his Old Testament counterpart; he acts as a moral touchstone for those around him. Just as the biblical Nathan rebuked David for murdering a man to marry his wife, Nathan Landau rebukes the world for the most monstrous horror of the twentieth century— the Holocaust. Nathan is quite literally mad with the knowledge of Auschwitz and is determined to make those around him as obsessed and demonic as he. Although never touched literally by the European genocidal madness, he understands how nobody, Jew or Gentile, can escape the ramifications and consequences of the Holocaust. Although Nathan is literally diagnosed as schizophrenic, we must see his fragmentation and rage as a necessary response to the excruciating horrors the twentieth century has wrought. The biblical Nathan's advice helped save Solomon's kingdom; similarly, Nathan Landau's warnings about the evil that is totalitarianism must be heeded if this planet is to survive. Nathan Landau, then, is prophet and moral touchstone, a Jew sickened by the mass murder of the family of Jews. Nathan embodies Hitler's jibe: "Conscience is a Jewish invention."

There is also the other side of Nathan, the destructive one. Nathan has delusions of grandeur, imagining himself a great Nobel Prize-winning scientist, able to rid the world of polio. This Landau is, unfortunately, nothing like Lev Landau, the Russian Jewish physicist, who did win the Nobel Prize. Nathan would like to destroy a killer virus and extinguish all evil, but it is his obsession with ridding the world of evil that destroys those around him, including himself. Being maniacal about totalitarianism produces, ironically, totalitarian behavior; Nathan can act with brutality, can become authoritarian, usurping the rights of others, can demean those whom he loves. Nathan is blinded by his cause, by his own self-righteousness, very much like an earlier Nathan, Nat Turner, a man whose strong sense of morality provoked immorality and violence.

Nathan has his own form of survivor guilt to haunt him—a Jew who never had to ride one of the crowded trains to a concentration camp, a Jew protected merely by his geographic location. That is part of the reason he is so enraged by a Gentile's having survived the camps. So many Jews perished, why should a Gentile survive, and by extension, why should Nathan survive when his brothers did not? In battering Sophie, then, he is battering himself, displacing some of his own guilt. Their joint suicide makes total psychological sense; both are unable to bear the burden of their knowledge and experience; the Holocaust has claimed Jewish and Gentile victims, European and American bodies and souls, and forms of it continue to plague humanity in all parts of the globe. It is all too easy, too human, to succumb to totalitarian madness.

All this should serve as a rebuttal to the view that Nathan Landau is an anti-Semitic creation. Nathan is not just a Jew who is a torturer, a despicable character who demeans and destroys Sophie. Nathan is also a victim of the twentieth century, a victim of his own isolation and madness. To suggest that Nathan's destroying the Gentile Sophie is a case of Styron's "goyish revenge" is absurd. Nathan is not the demonic Jew whom all Gentiles fear but a man no longer able to believe in humanity's redemption; neither Sophie nor Nathan is able to conquer grief and despair. The "war against the Jews" in Europe destroyed the Polish Catholic Sophie, and Nathan's private war against those who perpetrated the "war against the Jews" destroys Sophie and himself. The name Sophie means wisdom, and Landau is a German town. Wisdom about the Nazis is indeed a wisdom that is woe, and for Sophie and Nathan, a woe that is madness. Nathan's sadism, then, must be interpreted broadly and not as a reflection of Styron's supposed anti-Semitism or the unconscious revenge of Jew against Gentile. It is, therefore, ironic that critics ignore Styron's portrait of Nathan's brother, Larry, a Jewish doctor who loves and protects his younger brother and helps heal Sophie, the ravished Gentile. Larry is the embodiment of the loving, educated, cultured, compassionate Jew.

It is obvious that *Sophie's Choice* explores the evil of anti-Semitism without itself being anti-Semitic; indeed, an examination of Styron's attitudes towards Jews and Jewish culture and a look at the Jewish fictional characters he has been creating for thirty years reveals a particular love and respect for and even identification with the Jews: philo-Semitism rather than anti-Semitism. We must remember that Styron is by birth a Southern WASP and as such was subjected to a certain dose of anti-Semitism, though of a much less virulent type than its European counterpart. Anti-Semitism in Southern society, nevertheless, is depicted in Styron's first novel, *Lie Down in Darkness*. The most moral character in that novel, however, is a

Northern Jew. The earliest of Styron's fiction, then, reveals his rebellion against his Wasp upbringing, his distaste for Christian hypocrisies and pretensions. All of Styron's fictional Jews are portrayed as moral touch-stones, outsiders, and rebels, not victims. It is the Jew who opts for a full life, for hope despite society's attempt to stifle creativity and individuality. If Jews suffer, they do not suffer as victims but as rebels made stronger by their suffering, a strength which helps them act on the behalf of others. Styron's Jews, then, testify to the dignity of humanity and to the affirmation of life.

What is, finally, so ironic about the charges of anti-Semitism against Styron and his novel is that *Sophie's Choice* is Styron's most Jewish book. It is not simply because the novel's subject is the Holocaust or because some of its characters and its setting are Jewish. What Styron has success-fully captured is Jewish sensibility, an ironic comic mode passed down from Sholem Aleichem to Bellow, Malamud, and Roth, novelists whom Styron admires. Styron has characterized the Jewish sensibility as "that comic awareness so exquisitely poised between hilarity and anguish" (Ruderman 138). This comic mode, adopted as a defense against tragedy, is the appro-priate one for *Sophie's Choice,* a novel itself poised between hilarity and anguish, between Stingo's gropings and Sophie's descent into hell. (For a more complete analysis of Styron's relationships with Jews and the use of Jewish fictional characters in his work, see Judith Ruderman's book, *Wil-liam Styron* [New York: Ungar, 1987], 129–39.)

What is critical is that Styron is able to capture Jewish sensibility because of his Southern roots, for Southerners, like Jews, carry the weight of a tragic history. Jewish novelists and some Southern novelists—Faulkner particularly comes to mind here—can acknowledge a tragic past while af-firming human dignity. Nathan predicted that the Jewish urban novel would supersede the Southern novel; Styron is the rich embodiment of these two great literary traditions.

To be a mainstream American writer, argues Jules Chametzky in *Our Decentralized Literature: Cultural Mediations in Selected Jewish and Southern Writers,* takes an audacious and appropriating act of the imagina-tion. A mainstream writer must be able to transcend limitations of region, or ethnic, gender, or class particularity, must transform the provincial and regional into the major and the universal. Before the Second World War, Southern and Jewish writers were considered marginal.

The subtlety of Styron's achievement, like Twain's and Roth's, lies in the awareness that the ground tends to shift, is not a fixed place in time or geography, ethnically or any other way, but rather depends on the flexibility, wit, and awareness of the writer as adapter and projector of various mediations and negotiations. (Chametzky 16)

Styron is able to assimilate the real marginals—Jews, blacks, and women—into the mainstream by appropriating their domain, thereby legitimating their experience. Because of this, Styron's stand-in, Stingo, is the appropriate sympathetic narrator for Sophie's and Nathan's tragic tales.

We have come full circle. Just as Elie Wiesel has dedicated his 1986 Nobel Peace Prize to the survivors of the Nazis for teaching "humankind how not to succumb to despair," Styron's *Sophie's Choice* shows us how through laughter and love we might begin the conquest of grief and despair.

3

Sex in Mid-Century America:
"A Nightmarish Sargasso Sea of Guilts and
Apprehension"

Sophie's Choice is set in what Styron calls the "frozen sexual moonscape of the 1940s," that "sexually bedeviled era." This time frame is crucial to the mood and meaning of the novel, to a fuller appreciation of what Styron accomplishes in *Sophie's Choice*. Some critics, however, have called the novel pornographic or at least too preoccupied with sex, particularly Stingo's masturbatory fantasies. Other critics think it inappropriate or in poor taste to contrast Stingo's sexual yearnings with Sophie's descent into hell, arguing that this minimizes Sophie's anguish and trivializes the Holocaust. Still others decry the portrait of Sophie as essentially sexist, indicting Stingo's limited male perspective and his desire for Sophie as obviating any objectivity in his narrative, thereby also diminishing Sophie's anguish. By extension, some critics call Styron a sexist because he does not allow Sophie to speak for herself but rather through a male interpreter, Stingo, Styron's stand-in. Some contemporary feminists are particularly at odds with Styron, who they feel creates only weak, dependent, deceitful, suicidal women. Issues involving sex and sexism in the novel, then, have created as much controversy as issues involving anti-Semitism and the appropriateness of fictionalizing the Holocaust at all.

Let us explore the charges of sexism first. Gloria Steinem, a leading feminist spokeswoman and founding editor of *Ms.* magazine, lambasted the novel in her 1981 *Ms.* review. It is worth quoting extensively from this review in order to understand the feminist view of Styron's supposed misogyny and his therefore inevitable sexist portrait of Sophie:

> By putting a woman into the title of his novel, William Styron (author/narrator/protagonist) might encourage readers to believe that he could write about a woman with empathy.... He brings the same liberal *chutzpah* and infuriating bias to her portrayal.
>
> For instance, though Sophie had been strong enough to survive the deaths of her two

children and years of atrocities in a concentration camp, though she vowed to (and does) live longer than its hated commandant so that he will not triumph, she is described by Styron as freely choosing to love a sexual fascist in New York; a drug addict who beats her and is so jealous that he literally condemns her for living.

There could be alternative explanations: this man saved her life with medical treatment for malnutrition, and besides, she has almost zero alternatives. Nonetheless, the author/narrator rebukes her for expressing relief when her violent lover temporarily takes off. Though the narrator professes to love Sophie, and is (God knows) sexually obsessed with her, he also admires her sadistic lover. (What turns out to be the lover's long history of criminally insane behavior is seen by Styron as a fairly normal male mating style.) Alarm only sets in when the lover threatens to kill not just Sophie but the narrator, too.

Sophie's choice turns out to have been unthinkable: a Nazi officer had forced her to choose which child, her son or her daughter, might survive the gas ovens, and threatened to kill them both if she did not comply. She chose to save her son. Though Styron elaborates on the possible motive of the guard (he decides it was a religious desire to force a sinful choice), he spends *not one word* on the sexual politics and self-hatred of the choice of his title. Son-preference is expected; so much so, it needs no comment. It's as natural as sexual masochism in a woman.

And so is suicide. Like the heroine of his first novel, *Lie Down in Darkness,* Sophie chooses to kill herself. (Another unexamined motive is why she does this in preference to being "saved" by marriage to the Styron character. He just assumes that she was irretrievably doomed.) Either Styron prefers suicidal heroines, or prospective heroines have been reading his books.

Though the events of Sophie's life conform to the author's misogyny in a way that makes me suspicious, I'm willing to believe that there was a real Sophie and that his memory of her is accurate. The problem is that he just takes for granted female self-hatred, egolessness, and obsession with pleasing men. The reader comes away convinced that, if she weren't beautiful and the author hadn't spent a whole summer trying to go to bed with her, he wouldn't have bothered to record her experience at all.

Of course, there's always the hope that the movie of *Sophie's Choice* won't be as painful as the book. But I had the same fantasy while reading about Sophie as I did while reading Styron's version of Turner. If she were still alive, she might mount a campaign of signs and graffiti: "Please help me. I am a prisoner in a book by William Styron." (Steinem 27)

It would be fair to note here that years earlier, in 1972, Styron revealed in an interview for *Esquire* that while the immediate aims of the women's liberation movement did not offend him, the "shrill scream" of many did. In particular, he singled out Steinem, calling her "practically illiterate" and "a terrible opportunist who will don any fashionable garb so long as it's in vogue. I think her history has proved that" (Halpern 143). It is not surprising, then, that Steinem's review of *Sophie's Choice* would be critical. Beyond the personal enmity, however, are issues that must be addressed—Styron's/Stingo's misogyny—for some male critics have agreed with Steinem's assessment of the novel, and feminists, in general, argue that interpreting language is no more sexually neutral than language or the language system itself.

One such male critic is William Heath, who attacked the novel in an article called "I, Stingo: The Problem of Egotism in *Sophie's Choice*." He argues that the novel's title should have been *Stingo's Progress* since he sees it as a dramatization of Stingo's narcissism, which sabotages Sophie's tragedy. Heath sees Stingo as an exploiter, using Sophie for material for his novel and to proclaim himself a Great Lover and Great Writer. In short, Heath calls Stingo an unreliable narrator who does not know himself.

Similarly, critic Michael Kreyling in an article called "Speakable and Unspeakable in Styron's *Sophie's Choice*" argues that language is the medium and the subject of the book, that men have appropriated Sophie through the imposition of a superior language: Kreyling is referring to Sophie's father, Höss, Nathan, and Stingo. In particular, Kreyling criticizes Stingo and male writers whose "priapic urges and verbal libido are phrases or aspects of [their] foreordained calling to sow the world with meaning" (553). Stingo tells Sophie's story, and Nathan corrects Sophie's English, ridiculing her errors at times.

From the feminists to some male critics, Stingo/Styron has been seen as a pathetic egotist, a chauvinist exploiting Sophie's tragedy. This argument about how a man can speak for or write convincingly about a woman parallels the argument outlined earlier—how a nonsurvivor can write about the Holocaust. Contrary to these critics, it can be shown that Styron is not a sexist, and that Stingo is not an exploiter but the appropriate narrator for Sophie's tragic tale, that the portrayal of the sexual troubles in the post-Holocaust era is crucial to the meaning of *Sophie's Choice*.

Recently, in an article about the movie *Tin Men* which appeared in *The New York Times,* the movie's writer and director, Barry Levinson, said, "In the age of the 'sensitive man,' the male writer who exposes ... unpleasant truths often gets branded a sexist or misogynist for his troubles.... You're criticized for believing in the things that you're just trying to illustrate" (Freedman). *Tin Men* dramatizes the tremendous gulf separating men and women. Set in the pre-Vietnam, pre-women's liberation 1960s, this movie about aluminum-siding salesmen in Baltimore demonstrates that men's desire for women is equaled only by their disdain for them. Like Levinson, Styron is criticized for believing in things that he is just trying to illustrate.

In a 1983 *Psychology Today* interview, editor James Ellison asked Styron to comment on the negative feminist reaction to his portrayal of Sophie on the grounds that she is too weak, too much the victim. Styron responded:

> I would say that there's something wrong with anyone who felt that Sophie was an ill-spirited portrait of a woman. I fail to see any place in the book that could offend a reader's idea of femaleness or womanhood. And, in addition, at the risk of overanalyzing

my own work, I don't know of a woman in modern literature who has suffered as much at the hands of men as Sophie has. Her father is a monster, her husband is a monster, her male associates in the camp are monsters, and finally, she is done to death by a haphazardly monstrous but nonetheless terrifying psychopath. It is true that Sophie responded to men in certain masochistic and supine ways, but that was simply the way she was constituted, and anyone who would construe that as an insult to womanhood is just simply a lunatic. I don't know what women want. (Ellison)

When asked if he felt his treatment of women had undergone any change through the increasingly feminist climate of the 1970s, Styron answered:

It's very hard for me to step back and examine analytically my professional attitude toward women. But I have found that true women—not feminist harpies—have responded to my work in a very strong way, starting with *Lie Down in Darkness*. I've saved most of the letters written to me, and I think that if any disgruntled feminist radical would go through them, she would realize that my work has had a strong and positive effect on women. Women have been centrally located in almost all my work. And they have almost always been victims—victims of men. (Ellison)

Shortly after that conversation with James Ellison, Styron was interviewed by Judith Thurman in *Mademoiselle* about a male writer's ability to write convincingly about females. Thurman asked Styron how a man is able to write intimately about a woman. Styron replied:

I can't say precisely how a male writer is able to create a woman character. There are fragments in Sophie of many women I have known. But the fact is, we all have components of maleness and femaleness in us, and I am able to draw on a certain femaleness in me to describe this woman, from the inside, as she is meant to be. . . . In the beginning, I didn't actually conceive of Sophie as being so subservient, if that's the word—so masochistic in her relationships with men. But I soon saw that that was an important component of how I had to tell the story. She was victimized by men all her life. . . . When you are creating a special person, you cannot make apologies. You simply have to show her the way she is, to render her tragedy and to do it justice. (Thurman 159)

Thurman then asked Styron what he understands about the relationship between sexuality and violence. Styron said:

It has always bewildered me why men are violent. But this does not prevent me from perceiving how—perhaps out of the little flickers I might have in my own being—how this violence could erupt in certain men. . . . If you are really honest, you have to admit that the violence exists—both in men toward women and in women toward themselves. Many of Sophie's masochistic sexual fantasies were confessed to me by real women. Women give male writers their most interesting secrets, you know. (Thurman 204)

Thurman then wondered why Styron seems to kill off the women he really cares about. Styron answered:

It is nothing more complicated than having a tragic view of the human condition. I suppose I could write some kind of story in which the heroic woman becomes a symbol for survival. But women and men are victims . . . of being half-connected animals. Who live neither in nature nor in civilization. Who don't know how to accommodate either one. Nor do most men and women seem able to accommodate each other, to find an equilibrium within a love affair or a marriage. . . . Perhaps the tragedy, the flaw, is the romantic notion that everything can be perfect or is perfectible. In reality it is a struggle. (Thurman 204)

Thurman then questioned Styron about how his intimacy with a character, with Sophie, over many years affects his relations with real people in his life, with his wife, for example. Styron responded:

I think it enhances those relations. I have the feeling that creating Sophie was, in fact, an act of catharsis for me which allowed me, once again, to enter a state of balance with the opposite sex. I think it was a healthy thing for me to do. I saw, in effect, that I could create a full-blown—another persona for myself. In other words, I dragged out of that femaleness in me, which all men have somewhere, a living human being. It satisfied the desire for a new birth in myself and a new birth out of myself. And I felt a great jolt, a sense of confidence and recognition which had been eluding me before. (Thurman 204)

Shortly before these interviews, in 1982, *Esquire* magazine published a series of conversations between Styron and the actress Candice Bergen. Bergen remarked that she marvels at the fact that Styron has been married so long and so well to Rose Burgunder, acknowledging that Rose is "one of the great women of our time" ("A Conversation" 91). (Rose is a poet and Amnesty International activist.) Styron said of his wife:

Yes, she is an exceptional woman, which only makes it tougher, you know. In a curious way, she is so extraordinary you feel your own sense of inadequacy in the face of it. . . . It's very hard to live with a person who is extremely good. It really is. Your own character is always being unconsciously called into question. ("A Conversation" 91)

Bergen then asked him if living with a good person improved his own character. Styron said:

Yes, it also does that. One realizes that, reflected against basic decency and goodness, one's own conduct is wanting badly. I knew Camus, never knew his wife, but apparently he was married to an extremely fine woman. He said it was a cross he had to bear because his own character was always being put to the test. ("A Conversation" 91)

From these interviews alone, we would be hard pressed to call Styron a sexist or misogynist. In exposing anti-Semitism, Styron was accused of being anti-Semitic himself. For exposing unpleasant truths about the relationship between the sexes, he had been branded a sexist. Anyone who has read *Sophie's Choice* can never forget his portrait of Sophie; she is one of the richest, most multidimensional heroines in modern American literature. In a review of the novel in *Commentary* in 1979, shortly after the novel's publication, Pearl Bell wrote:

> With a sure instinct, Styron has written Sophie's story in the grand manner of 19th-century fiction—she is, indeed, one of the very few women in contemporary American fiction to possess something of the tragic stature and self-defeating complexity of such classic heroines as Tolstoy's Anna Karenina and Hardy's Sue Bridehead. A victim of absolute evil, she is not simply a pathetic survivor trembling before the lash of fate. She is lover, liar, masochist, drunk—a martyr but not a saint. Despite the cowardice and deception she divulges to Stingo, it is impossible not to be touched by the nobility of this lovable woman devoured by self-loathing. Even when she summons up the courage to tell her young friend, with self-flagellating candor, about her pretense of anti-Semitism when making a futile attempt to seduce Rudolf Höss, the commandant of Auschwitz, while working as his secretary, we cannot bring ourselves to condemn Sophie. The cruel secret hidden in the title is withheld until almost the last, and it is the darkest reason of all for Sophie's suppurating guilt. In Sophie Zawistowska, Styron has achieved an intensity of feeling and pain that is admirably unsentimental, and he forces us to see that her sins deserve, beyond pity, the generosity of forgiveness. (Bell 58)

Richard Pearce, a critic who has written a full-length study on Styron's novels called *William Styron,* says about Sophie that until she meets Nathan she is quite ordinary and cowardly. But through Nathan she develops a thirst for life, the capacity for guilt, and an attraction to death which gives her tragic stature. Nathan forces Sophie to confront the madness of the Holocaust and her own involvement in it. In our post-Holocaust era to have created a heroine thought to have tragic stature, a heroine compared to an Anna Karenina or a Sue Bridehead, is more than tribute enough to the greatness of Styron's creation. Like Anna and Sue, Sophie is both intelligent and alluring, crushed by the weight of societal injustices as well as by her own individual tragic flaws. Curiously, all three heroines defy society's rigid feminine stereotypes, all three being devoted mothers *and* passionate lovers in patriarchal cultures.

Sophie's Choice, then, is not sexist but a novel which explores sexism, a form of oppression. In a provocative article entitled "Styron's *Sophie's Choice:* The Structure of Oppression," Carolyn Durham, professor of French, contends that sexism illuminates all forms of oppression, that what Styron reveals in the novel is essentially a globally sexist world. The lower status of women represents systematic oppression. Styron has always been interested in what he sees as the propensity for human beings to dominate one another, the prevalence of master-slave relationships in human affairs. Styron uses the condition of women, then—women as the second or subordinate sex—as the central metaphor for the general degradation of self and

others. Sophie is a price, an object, to every man. She has always understood the necessity of female submission in a male-dominated world just
as her mother before her understood her role in Cracow. In this context, it
can be argued that Sophie unconsciously chose to have her daughter, Eva,
murdered by the Nazis rather than her son, Jan. Eva (Eve) must be punished
for having tasted the forbidden fruit from the tree of knowledge, tempting
Adam, causing their exile from the Garden of Eden. Eve, ironically, means
life in Hebrew, yet Eva is murdered, and Sophie will murder herself.
Women are punished for their knowledge and wisdom (and the name So-
phia means wisdom). Sophie knows from experience that life would be
harder for Eva, indeed any female, than for Jan. Unfortunately, victimization causes self-hatred, a hatred which should more appropriately be directed towards her oppressors.

Styron dramatizes for us the evils of sexism on many levels. Sophie is
still overly tied to her tyrannical, dead father and in death joins him, yet she
is more like her sweet self-effacing mother. Her choice to have Eva murdered is further proof that sexism is potentially lethal, that women often
view themselves as expendable, as having little choice and power in a patriarchal society; indeed, many women have either gone mad or killed themselves as the only way out of a sexist world. Sophie was a very intelligent
woman who was, nevertheless, a secretary to three men: her father, Höss,
and Blackstock. Sophie was forced to transcribe the vile thoughts of her
rabid, anti-Semitic father and those of Commandant Höss, transcribing his
"Final Solution" orders. Unfortunately, Sophie could not find a way to say
no to these men, always needing the loving approval of the one and the
other's benevolence in order to survive. The origin of female oppression in
Sophie's Choice is clearly seen in father dominance. Even Sophie's sexual
fantasies reveal her need to be overtaken, to submit to the power of male
dominance. This is partially responsible for her undoing, for her tragic
ending. To rebel against sexism, against domination, however, takes a
strong will; the individual is responsible for the liberation of the self. Sophie
lacks this will and chooses instead to enslave herself, a choice which contributes to her tragic ending.

Durham feels that the novel's meaning lies in its structure, in the concept of structure itself. The opening chapter about Stingo's stint as an editor
for McGraw-Hill already reveals the kinds of oppression that will hover
over this novel. Stingo cannot conform, cannot be the ideal organization
man in terms of his clothing (he will not wear a hat) or what he reads
(Stingo prefers the then radical *New York Post* and *The Daily Worker* to
the more conservative *Herald Tribune,* although he is told that sensationalism is preferable to radicalism). Stingo is fired for the heinous crime of
blowing bubbles out of his office window. Important, too, is the fact that

this large organization, this bureaucracy, is clearly male-dominated: the men are the editors who make the decisions and the women are their secretaries. So, contrary to the argument that the opening chapter is too autobiographical, or too self-indulgent, even irrelevant to Sophie's story, the opposite is true; the first chapter telegraphs the novel's themes.

The organization man is shown as the root of all evil, conforming to all the rules, obeying male authority figures. Bureaucracy is a system geared to oppose and oppress any individuality. Stingo was able to rebel against this system, preserving his individuality. Sophie, and women by extension, however, receive protection and their identities at the expense of their self-esteem, paying the price of a childlike dependence on men. Sylvia Black-stock, Sophie's employer's wife, is described as a "doll," a doctor's idle wife who shops and drinks too much; there is no constructive outlet for her. Sylvia's inebriation contributes to her having a bizarre car accident which decapitates her, a bitter metaphor for women's directionless, power-less position in a patriarchal culture.

Stingo, however, is enslaved in a patriarchal culture as well. His need to assert his masculinity by losing his virginity, by lusting after Leslie Lapidus and Sophie, is seen as both comic and tragic. Women do become a means to an end in a society which emphasizes the conquest of women, the diminishing of women into sexual objects who boost men's egos; Stin-go's sexual fantasies, therefore, demonstrate Styron's awareness that sexism degrades both men and women, of how it turns love into lust and healthy sexuality into lechery. *Sophie's Choice* reveals a sexually troubled, post-Holocaust world, where sexuality is influenced by oppressive forms of domination and submission, with sado-masochistic elements, where power not tenderness dominates heterosexual coupling. In exposing this unpleas-ant truth, that men's desire is often equal to their disdain for women, Styron has been stamped a sexist or misogynist for his troubles; actually, in expos-ing the evils of sexism, Styron is hoping to undermine this oppression, not applaud it.

There are, of course, other critics who argue that *Sophie's Choice* is not only not sexist, but that Stingo is the perfect narrator for Sophie's story even though the older narrator acknowledges that the young Stingo can go only so far in understanding Sophie or the Holocaust. The tone of the narration resembles that in James Joyce's "Araby," slightly mocking and derisive; indeed, we are told at the very beginning of the novel that the nickname Stingo, deriving from Stinky, mysteriously disappeared when Stingo was in his thirties. Stingo at twenty-two, however, is young and arrogant enough to begin his tale with "Call me Stingo," forcing the reader to compare him with Melville's Ishmael and his great voyage of discovery. Stingo is a "lean and lonesome young Southerner wandering amid the

Kingdom of the Jews," imagining himself "a writer with the same ardor and the soaring wings of the Melville or the Flaubert or the Tolstoy or the Fitzgerald" who summoned him to their incomparable vocation. Stingo, however, is aware of a "large hollowness" within him, a man whose "spirit has remained landlocked, unacquainted with love and all but a stranger to death." His "smug and airless self-deprivation" would soon be disturbed and altered forever in Brooklyn, but it is not until long after Sophie's death that Stingo understands her and himself better. With these limitations in mind, it is critical to see why Stingo *is* the appropriate sympathetic narrator for Sophie's story, that he is more than a mercenary exploiter or pathetic egotist; Stingo has an abundance of male empathy for females.

While Stingo does have a youthful, brash confidence, he nevertheless carries within him his own demons. Stingo at thirteen experienced the early and slow death from cancer of his mother. He learns of the suicide of his childhood girlfriend, Maria Hunt, and, of course, is grief stricken by the loss of his two best friends, Nathan and Sophie. Stingo lives with his own form of survivor guilt, feeling guilty that he was unable to forestall disaster, unable to prevent the untimely deaths of these three women. Stingo tries to understand and identify and empathize with females and, moreover, to express and explain that empathy, fearing that he has failed them. The truth is, however, that through his imagination Stingo effectively enters Sophie's mind and heart so well that for long stretches in the novel we hear Sophie's voice; that is, her voice actually takes over. Stingo has saved Sophie imaginatively for us. Those familiar with Styron's first novel, *Lie Down in Darkness,* will remember Peyton Loftis' haunting, presuicide monologue in which a male narrator imaginatively enters the psyche of a despairing woman.

There are other important parallels between Stingo and Sophie which enable him to empathize with her. First, both are lonely and love-starved Gentiles in the Kingdom of the Jews. Both are attracted to Nathan's glamour and generosity, and both are abused by Nathan's demonic side. They both share some guilt over the genocidal past of their countries: Poland's anti-Semitism and the American South's tragic history of racism. They both need to overcome stereotyped notions about Jews and blacks. Stingo and Sophie are also nominal Christians, having lost their faith some years earlier. Sophie also has what Stingo desires—a lusty, fulfilling sexual relationship, an uninhibited heterosexual union.

More than their love for Nathan, it is their survivor guilt which haunts them, which unites them psychologically and spiritually. They have both experienced the death of close loved ones (Sophie on a wider scale, of course), and both feel guilty for not forestalling disaster and for surviving at all. The survivor always feels he or she could have done more, was selfish, was responsible for the death of a loved one. In Sophie's case, she was forced to decide which of her children would be murdered by the Nazis. Stingo felt that his selfishness inadvertently led to his mother's death and subsequently feels the need to "rescue" other women from disastrous fates. This need to rescue was successful only in Stingo's artistic recreation of Sophie's story, for the women he loved, his mother, Maria, and Sophie, all die.

This subtle psychological sympatico takes some interesting forms. First, music is an integral part of the lives and stories of both Stingo and Sophie. Music is seen as life-affirming, as restorative, to both of them. It is music which has the power to rescue Sophie from her suicidal despair, although it is powerless in the face of death; Stingo is ecstatic in the Pink Palace partially because of Nathan's extensive record collection and eagerly tells Sophie on their ride to the South that the first thing they will do when they get to Virginia is to buy some albums. Both need to listen to classical music, both are capable of appreciating its grandeur, dignity, and sensuality; indeed, Styron himself listens to classical music to put him in an exalted frame of mind before he can settle down to write.

Also important is Styron's use of dreams in *Sophie's Choice* to unite the narrator and the tale. Professor Daniel Ross presented a paper entitled "Dreams and the Two Plots in Styron's *Sophie's Choice*" at the Styron Symposium at Winthrop College in Rock Hill, South Carolina, in April 1986 which demonstrates how Stingo's and Sophie's dreams reveal their similar anxieties embedded in their unconscious lives. Stingo and Sophie, in Freudian language, have some unresolved Oedipal ties. Both experienced the death of their opposite sex parent. Both have some guilt about these deaths, desiring some punishment for their supposed "waywardness." Their dreams reveal frustrated erotic feelings as well as guilt over not pleasing their opposite sex parent, and a desperate need for their love and approval. Sophie does eventually return to that symbiotic relationship with her father in death. Although some part of Sophie hates her father and everything he stands for, feels almost suffocated by him, she will allow herself to yield to her self-destructiveness, in effect pleasing her father by her suicide. Stingo, however, does not go back to the father and will give up the notion of an idyllic existence in the South; that is, Stingo will learn not to idealize his parents blindly, will cut the umbilical cord. He comes to terms with his guilt and childish dependence although he struggles regularly with his fear of failing women and their failing him. He does rescue Sophie from drowning but not ultimately from suicide. Both Stingo and Sophie are orphans of sorts. The great essayist De Quincey once said, "It is, or it is not, according to the nature of men, an advantage to be orphaned at an early age" (in Simpson, epigraph). It is potentially for Stingo; it is not for Sophie.

Their dreams, then, reveal the human tendency to punish oneself for unpreventable deaths. Sophie feels guilty for not complying, and Stingo feels guilty for not rescuing, which leaves both of them lonely and frightened, desiring punishment. The biggest difference is that Stingo is the lone survivor able to tell the tale because he is able to conquer grief and guilt, to mourn fully, to come to grips with the tragic compulsion towards self-destruction which arises from the need to recreate the same undesired state of affairs endured as a child—feeling either unloved or unlovable. In the Prussian culture, tyrannical parents were idealized and honored; battering children was a standard child-rearing practice. Many of the men who surrounded Hitler were battered children themselves.

Ross continued his exploration of *Sophie's Choice* in a paper entitled "Sophie's Case, or What Does a Man Want?" delivered at the Feminism and Psychoanalysis Conference at Illinois State University, May 3, 1986. Ross argues that the novel is more a case history than a *Bildungsroman*. A case history describes the tension between male and female, hero and heroine, teller and tale. Ross compares the relationship between Stingo and Sophie to the famous Freud/Dora relationship. Stingo, like Freud, usurps center stage, but the tragic tales of Sophie and Dora gain power because of their effect on the male auditors/narrators who reconstitute themselves as a result of their relationships with their "heroines." This is in no way a diminishing of strength since Ross believes case histories can be great works of literature.

It is true that Stingo acts as Sophie's confessor, that his limitations distort her story. Stingo's need to resolve his own Oedipal conflict, his guilt over his mother's suffering, and his desire for manhood through sexual initiation limit his understanding of Sophie. In short, Stingo is not neutral towards Sophie; his lust for her often overwhelms his compassion for her. Freud was not neutral towards Dora either. Stingo is a victim of his innocence as well as a victim of the culture that ingrained the mystique of manhood in him. Stingo feels he must assert his power over women to be a man, but his privileged status includes an obligation to take care of women. And Sophie is driven to please her tyrannical and unloving father, a model she repeats with all men. Sophie is a victim of all men, even men who try to help her, because their prejudices and desires distort their ability to help. It is only after Sophie's death that Stingo learns how to read Sophie and make sense out of his own life.

It is crucial here to maintain the distinction between the older narrator and his youthful alter ego. We witness self-hatred in Sophie and Stingo, a by-product of our patriarchal culture which provides erroneous assumptions about sexuality, aggression, and domination, exacting a high price from men and women. Stingo learns that maturity and manhood mean more than sexual conquest and gratification, and he learns this partially because of Sophie, who refuses to be "protected" by a marriage to Stingo, who shows him that sometimes sex is a way to "beat back death," a "flight from memory and grief." Sophie teaches him the meaning of "unearned unhappiness," makes him understand the absolute urgency of conquering grief without which only madness or death follows, that only love can conquer evil. Ross argues that *Sophie's Choice* is about sexism, is an indictment of our patriarchal culture, but is not sexist itself. If anything, it is the woman, sphinxlike, who has the knowledge to impart to the man, the woman whose experience transforms male consciousness.

This argument is not the same as saying Stingo exploited Sophie's anguish to become a better artist. It is true her life and death help him write his novel at a time when he "had the syrup but it wouldn't pour," but more importantly Sophie's story changes the kind of person Stingo becomes when he sheds the nickname Stingo and becomes a man, much less innocent but not without "some fragile yet perdurable hope," a man no longer a stranger to love and death, no longer hollow.

The feminist movement has come a long way in the last few years—a fact made evident if we contrast Steinem's attitudes, which reflect an earlier stage of the women's movement, with a 1987 book by Claudia Koonz called *Mothers in the Fatherland: Women, the Family and Nazi Politics,* nominated for a National Book Award. Koonz argues that for the Nazi plan to have worked, women had to have been collaborators in a system clearly misogynist. She shows how Nazi women paradoxically ended up destroying the family they swore to uphold. Middle-class women in Protestant, Catholic, charitable, and even women's rights associations all marched into the new regime, yet they had no real power. Koonz also chronicles the stories of women who risked their lives against a government they defined as evil. Women, then, were fanatical followers, victims, and resisters of the Third Reich, proving that no sex has a premium on either good or evil. Women are not necessarily morally or emotionally superior to men, a message that needs to be incorporated into feminist thinking. Even though this book explores a dark aspect of women's past, Koonz urges us to learn to "beware those who would create a segmented society. And beware calls to revive so-called old-fashioned womanhood and subordination to men—appeals to crude, nostalgic 'familyism'" (Collins).

Feminists are beginning to see that it is not enough to uncover old heroines or to imagine new ones, to attack patriarchy with its oppressive language. Feminists must attack the socio-sexual arrangements that keep us from our own potential and from each other. This attitude has already been expressed by French feminists. Styron does not take for granted "female self-hatred, egolessness, and obsession with pleasing men," as Steinem argues. What Styron does is show how patriarchal and sexist attitudes hurt both men and women, that sexism is a form of slavery and as such must be abhorred and struggled against; indeed, Styron shows how women are often the victims of men who are themselves victims of false values. Both men and women must act to end the domination without exacting new cruelties on new victims, a difficult view but ultimately the only liberating view.

Despite the fact that *Sophie's Choice* was written and published in the sexually liberal 1970s, there were still critics who thought the novel obscene, claiming there was too much sex in the novel in general, compromising the novel artistically. Some argued that the inclusion of sex at all was in poor taste in a novel about the Holocaust. The older narrator himself questions the inclusion of certain sexual scenes, particularly the extensive encounters with the teasing Leslie Lapidus and those with Mary Alice Grimball, a different sort of tease; yet the narrator chooses to include them, intuiting that they reveal the urgency and desperate eroticism of the 1940s, and that somehow their inclusion is important to the texture and meaning of the story. The word *obscene* takes on two meanings: the language and description of sexual frustration and longing, particularly its abundant autoeroticism, and the irreverence of including any sexuality in a novel about Auschwitz, prompting critic Alvin Rosenfeld to call *Sophie's Choice* "the erotics of Auschwitz." A closer look at the portrayal of sexuality in the novel reveals the utter necessity of the inclusion of the sexual scenes and language to help complete a portrait of an era, that "sexually bedeviled era" of the 1940s, with ramifications for contemporary readers. As Styron insists, a novel can possess a significance apart from its subject matter, so a story about Sophie and the Holocaust can say at least as much about longing and loneliness as it does about the Holocaust and evil. The purpose of the novel's explicit sexuality is certainly not to arouse our prurient interest, is not pornographic; the novel's desperate eroticism is meant to instruct rather than to delight us.

Sophie's Choice is a novel as much about sexual repression, about the "frozen sexual moonscape" as it is about the Nazis. The sexual urge when repressed often asserts itself perversely. It is all the more ironic, then, that a novel which seeks to reveal the devastating effects of sexual repression should have been turned into a sexually timid film produced in a supposedly more liberated America of the 1980s. The film whitewashes, to a large degree, the sado-masochistic sexuality between Nathan and Sophie. Styron, although generally impressed by the 1982 film version of his novel, and with Meryl Streep's performance in particular, was nonetheless disturbed by the omission of the novel's crucial sado-masochistic eroticism. In a 1983 interview, Styron said:

There was some sort of timidity, almost, which prevented the movie from touching on that very important area of the relationship between Sophie and Nathan. It vitiated the whole ending to my mind, because there is no premonition, as you get in the book, of why and how they're going to die together, by mutual suicide, by poisoning, not even a hint of that in the movie. (West 263)

It is four decades since the close of World War II, and despite blatant sexuality in our advertisements, in our television programs and films, despite the awful scourge of AIDS, America is still, on the whole, prudish and puritanical.

A further irony is revealed in the Russian translation of *Sophie's Choice*. In an interview in 1981 before the release of the movie, Styron spoke about the fact that his novel was translated into Russian by a woman from the KGB, but in the Russian edition, the part that has been translated to great fanfare was heavily edited. Styron recounted how the translator spent three hours editing through the love scenes which she found crude. The translator kept repeating: "Our people are very human; of course we behave the same way as your people . . . but . . . but it is against the law" (West 255). The Soviet Union has put an official block on the novel. How bitter that a novel which explores the connection between political and sexual brutality, between political and sexual repression, should be considered illegal in the Soviet Union, a country known for its own labor camps filled with political prisoners and censorship.

When asked why there is so much sexuality in the novel, Styron responded as follows in a 1983 interview:

Given the nature of the relationship between Sophie and Nathan, I think I would have been remiss had I not tried to explore the sado-masochistic eroticism that existed. Sophie and Nathan were possessed by some sort of demons that caused them to devour each other and that involved a great deal of erotic lunacy. After all, they did kill each other, and they had to come very close to the brink. As a metaphor, death and love have always been entwined in literature. The death wish and the procreative wish have often been so closely connected you can't separate them. That was essential to me and to the relationship between Sophie and Nathan. (West 262–63)

Their erotic violence (he kicks her, breaks her ribs, and tries to urinate in her mouth) was a mirror of the human degradation going on at Auschwitz daily. Here Styron links political and sexual fascism.

Styron demonstrates that Sophie's desirability is not the result of her being a mutilated person, not because she has come back from hell, but simply because she is a superb woman. This is not, as some critics have suggested, a sick novel about the excitement of sexually exploiting an already ravaged woman. That would not explain Stingo's attraction to Sophie. We must keep in mind that Nathan's sadism is drug- and madness-induced, an obvious contrast to the routine sadism that took place in the concentration camps, particularly the lesbian assaults on Sophie, where such actions were, if not legitimated, at least tolerated in that nightmare world.

On the other hand, we are reminded of the digital rape Sophie experienced in a darkened New York City subway car: the wanton randomness of the act does more to unnerve and unhinge Sophie than the lesbian assaults in Auschwitz. Submitting to the lesbian assaults was a matter of survival; being the random victim of digital rape by an anonymous assailant is more damaging psychically since it is a graphic reminder to Sophie of how little control she has over her life, how close she still is to that nightmare world of the camps from which she so desperately tries to escape. The subway rape demonstrates how women are often the victims of male sexual aggression, sexuality devoid of tenderness or mutuality. Such debasement of human sexuality can lead to psychic numbing and even, for some, to suicide, the victim punishing herself instead of the attacker; indeed, Sophie was suicidal after the digital rape. Only the majesty of Mozart's music prevented that, at least temporarily. Here Styron shows how death and love are closely entwined, how the death wish and the procreative urge are so closely connected that it is hard to separate them.

Since *Sophie's Choice* is a *Bildungsroman,* chronicling Stingo's journey of discovery, we must put to rest the issue of the inappropriateness of the sexual episodes in the novel. They do not compromise the novel but rather give greater resonance and force to the novel's themes.

The sexual scenes in the novel, then, serve many purposes: 1) they provide the symbolic setting in which the action of the novel can take solid form; 2) they provide a portrait of an era; 3) they contrast the physically repressive nature of modern American sexuality with Sophie's more joyous and liberated sexuality; 4) they provide comic relief; 5) they help to paint a picture of the narrator's emotional state and needs at the that time, his obsession with losing his virginity; 6) they reveal the connection between sexual and political repression; and 7) they reveal the link between religious and sexual repression—Sophie's early strict Catholicism and Stingo's Southern Calvinism must be challenged if they are to achieve their full potential. There is a delicious irony in the fact that to share the same hotel room with Sophie in Washington in 1947 Stingo pretends he is the Reverend Entwhistle and Sophie is his wife, and it is under this pretense that Stingo and Sophie share their first and last abandoned lovemaking session—with religion legitimating sexuality rather than repressing it.

At this point it would be instructive to explore Stingo's sexual attitudes and some of his sexual experiences in order to draw some conclusions about "that sexually bedeviled era." The Stingo we meet at the novel's inception is a cocky, inexperienced editor in New York fantasizing about "carnal-minded lady writers melting at his editorial acumen." Stingo, the technical virgin (he does not count his one experience with a prostitute in Charlotte, North Carolina, because he wore two condoms and did not ejaculate), is obsessed with losing his virginity. With no immediate available partner, Stingo is reduced to autoeroticism. The absence of sex in his life is not just an extraneous fact: it seems to aggravate his poverty and his lonely, outcast state. Stingo is a voyeur, looking out of his West 11th Street apartment, fantasizing that he is copulating with strangers and fraternizing with famous literati. Stingo at twenty-two is very much the voyeur in general; he has not experienced enough of life, love, and death yet to be otherwise. We are told that his living in the University Residence Club on West 11th Street reduced him to impotence. What is crucial in that opening chapter is that Stingo is a voyeur but longs desperately to taste real life, to experience healthy heterosexuality.

Most poignant is his acknowledgment that this lack of sexual connection produces a painful, unwanted solitude—a loneliness with a "merciless and ugly face." Reading, however, does provide Stingo with some erotic fulfillment. The older Stingo comments that other than reading only a happy marriage can keep loneliness at bay (there are no happy marriages in *Sophie's Choice*). The younger Stingo cannot possibly know this about marriage; Stingo is simply desperate to become a man, and that meant heterosexual coupling. His editing job at McGraw-Hill is so frustrating that it fills him with rage; Stingo finds he must fight the "desolate urge to masturbate." Here Styron suggests a correlation between modern alienation from self and community and "the desolate urge to masturbate."

Convinced he must leave McGraw-Hill in order to pursue a more creative existence, Stingo moves to cheaper quarters in Brooklyn where he is persuaded to rent a room in the Pink Palace because of its owner's broadmindedness. Yetta, the landlady, indicates that Stingo may have a girl in his room and a girl can have a guy in her room because "what's good for the gander is good for the goose ... and if there's one thing I hate, it's hypocrisy." This liberalism thrills the young Stingo, convincing him that the summer of 1947 will be one of "carnal fulfillment." A middle-aged Jewish woman is decrying the double standard, and poor Stingo knows he is but an "ineffective and horny Calvinist among all these Jews." Stingo is prepared for his summer of "carnal fulfillment"; he has a box of three-dozen rolled and lubricated Trojan condoms; it is, after all, the pre-pill era. Four decades later condoms will be the preferred contraceptive for a very different reason—AIDS. Stingo will not have that summer of "carnal fulfill-ment" and will learn that even some Northern Jewish women only sound liberated, are just as tied to the double standard as their male counterparts, an important part of his voyage of discovery.

The sex-starved Stingo is made physically ill when he realizes that he is residing beneath two people who copulate like "crazed wild animals." It so disturbs him that he reaches for an Alka-Seltzer. The sexual noises above him sometimes make him feel hungry. In short, his being a voyeur has a visceral effect on him. His heart sinks even further when Morris Fink tells him not to fantasize about the other women living in the Pink Palace because they go to their mothers on weekends. So, the one sexually active woman is taken, and the others are tied to their mothers. This is a low ebb in Stingo's state of mind. What he does not realize, however, is that he has not even begun to understand the meaning of the word *grief*.

It is at this point that Stingo receives a letter from his father about the suicide of Maria Hunt, twenty-two years old, Stingo's age. As was typical in the 1930s and 1940s, Stingo loved her passionately yet chastely, following the ancient chivalric code: adore the woman from afar—look but do not touch. Stingo wonders whether he could have prevented her suicide in New York. He is so troubled by her suicide that he dreams about Maria's importuning him lewdly and awakes from his "lascivious dream" just when Maria is about to perform fellatio. The older Stingo understands that most of his memorable adult dreams have dealt with either sex or death. There is guilt and frustration revealed in that dream and an interesting role reversal; it is the woman who is seducing the man, something Stingo would love but is also probably terrified of. He feels he has failed Maria, both emotionally and sexually. The dream also reveals Stingo's sexual passivity, his wanting to be magically relieved of the burden of his virginity with no risk of rejection.

This interjection about Maria's suicide and his adolescent infatuation with her is critical for his relationship with Sophie. When Stingo sees Sophie for the first time, she so resembles Maria physically and spiritually (they both look despairing) that he falls in love almost instantly with Sophie. Despite Sophie's emaciation, Stingo is excited by the "casual but forthright way her pelvis moved and her truly sumptuous rear end." Thinking about Sophie results in his finding himself close to "some droll phallic penetration . . . of his displaced pillow." Again, Stingo is a voyeur forced into autoeroticism. More important psychologically, however, is the association between Maria and Sophie—two beautiful but despairing women whom Stingo desires, loves, and ultimately loses. Part of his love for Sophie, then, stems from his unconscious need to recreate his relationship with Maria in the hope of getting it right the second time, which in this context means sexual fulfillment and emotional rescuing. Stingo needs to learn that it is not his role to save women, that the need stems from his neurotic guilt over his mother's death.

We must remember that the 1940s was an era when smoking was considered sophisticated, not dangerous, when masturbation was said to cause acne, warts, or madness, when people were embarrassed by public displays of affection. Stingo feels very uncomfortable with the public displays of affection exhibited by Nathan and Sophie, but their friendship makes him feel "close to total salvation." It was an era when records were very expensive, when the thought of all of Nathan's free records upstairs stirs Stingo as much if not more than "pink and nubile female flesh." Reading and listening to music are erotic activities for Stingo, his only sexual outlets—that is until Nathan promises to introduce him to a "hot dish" at Coney Island, Leslie Lapidus.

Some argue that the Leslie Lapidus episode is a tasteless, exaggerated, irrelevant digression. It is true that the episode is included partially for its comic relief, and Styron does seem to be having some fun with this scene, perhaps getting a bit carried away. The older Stingo questions the inclusion of this scene but decides that the Leslie episode does have "an elusive meaning." What it reveals is the desperate eroticism of the 1940s, that era which "encouraged the propinquity of the flesh but still forbad the flesh's fulfillment," a time when couples had access to large back seats of cars but when that access was frustrating because of the injunction that girls remain virgins until marriage. Sex in mid-century America, a "nightmarish Sargasso Sea of guilts and apprehension" is an appropriate metaphor for sex in our post-Holocaust world. Sargasso is a gulfweed, a noxious growth, not valued for its beauty, growing wild and rank, cumbering the ground and hindering the growth of superior vegetation. The Sargasso Sea is a tract of the North Atlantic Ocean where masses of this weed are found. The "guilts and apprehension," then, are like the Sargasso, hindering our more superior emotional and spiritual growth. Sex in mid-century America, not valued for its intrinsic beauty, becomes "wild and rank."

Stingo says he does not want or need to marry a virgin, that he does not "idealize femininity," does not categorize women as either virginal or whorish. However, he had never seen a woman entirely unclothed, having been a product of his own "Christian gentility with its aching repressions and restraints." He blames the nasty little Protestants, who have placed this embargo upon the flesh. Leslie Lapidus, that promiscuous virgin, is not included, then, just for comic relief; she broadens the spectrum of public moral responsibility and awareness, showing how modern sex echoes the range of dilemmas in a confused world. She fits in seriously, therefore, as well as comically.

It is with this sociological background that Stingo encounters Leslie

Lapidus, a voluptuous, bright, Jewish, dark-haired beauty who Stingo thought was a woman "free of the horrendous conventions and pieties that afflict this hypocritical culture of ours." He finds, however, that for all her verbal abandon, Leslie is the prototypical Jewish American Princess, immortalized later by Philip Roth, daddy's little girl who promises to remain a virgin until after the wedding. Naturally, Stingo is taken in by Leslie's oral expressiveness, impressed by her frequent quoting from Lawrence's *Lady Chatterley's Lover*, a book locked up in Stingo's university library. Again, Stingo is made physically ill after his frustrating encounter with Leslie, acknowledging that had Leslie been what she seemed, the entire narrative would have been different because he would have become her slave. Since she is just a tease, Stingo has time to become more involved with Sophie and Nathan. Of course, given the code of the times, Stingo lies and tells Nathan that he did have sex with Leslie, but Nathan knows he is lying and honorably chooses to say nothing. Stingo envisions the more mature Leslie a married, multiorgasmic mother, Stingo the lovelorn voyeur.

Another aspect of the "frozen sexual moonscape" is illustrated when Stingo's father visits him in New York. They both stay at the McAlpin Hotel where Stingo muses about his father's sexuality. "Did he ever get laid?" After all, his father had been a widower for nine years. Yet most Southerners and Americans of his vintage were "reticent, even secretive, about sex." That area of his father's life remains a mystery to Stingo. The lack of candor about sexual matters is seen as hurtful and alienating. It might have helped Stingo feel a little less alone had his father been able to share his loneliness and even sexual frustrations with him. While in the McAlpin, Stingo hears a couple copulating in the next room, a painful fate for Stingo which again leads him to masturbatory fantasies about Leslie, Maria, and Sophie, all of whom seemed dead to him, one literally, the other two symbolically. Stingo again wonders whether he was responsible for these "deaths." The older narrator comments that in a few short decades men would no longer have to eavesdrop behind closed doors, that for $5.00 they could witness any sexual act they wished. (With cable television and home video cassette recorders, one need never eavesdrop again.) Even the young Stingo knows, however, that the primordial sexual urge is a source too demandingly procreative to be satisfied by "some handy makeshift."

When Stingo is finally naked with Sophie on the beach, he is paralyzed as if "ten thousand Presbyterian Sunday School teachers had massed above Long Island in a minatory cloud, their presence resolutely disabling [his] fingers." The residual effects of Stingo's Calvinist upbringing rear their repressive head; the religious embargo against sexual fulfillment still toys with his psyche. He is so excited by his nearness to real female flesh that he embarrassingly ejaculates too quickly. Stingo longs to be initiated into the world of oral sex; Sophie, trying to minimize Stingo's embarrassment, changes the subject, leading Stingo to wonder, "Could women, then, so instantaneously turn off their lust like a light switch?" Stingo is venting his own frustration at feeling like a slave to his libido, with its nagging insistence on gratification. It appears to him that women are not slaves to this "primordial derangement." In the 1940s it was still felt that men were more aggressively sexual than women, that their needs had to be satisfied, that sex for women was a matter of duty to their husbands, a matter of reproduction only. Not until the end of the narrative does Stingo learn that women can be just as needy for sexual expression and fulfillment as men, just as driven; however, Stingo does not realize until after the narrative's conclusion that sex is more than healthy, raw passion, that it is sometimes a flight from memory, an attempt to beat back death.

It is important to note here that while Stingo achingly desires the beautiful Sophie, he plays the confessor rather than the sexual aggressor role when she is despairing or particularly vulnerable. After hearing Sophie's long recitals of the horrors of Auschwitz, Stingo is left "beyond any stirring of desire." Many critics have overlooked this aspect of Stingo's sexuality. He does not exploit Sophie's tragedy; Stingo can separate his libidinous energies from his empathic leanings, can place her pain above his own needs. That he thinks they could be a happily married couple on a peanut farm is more a matter of his naivete than his insensitivity; Stingo is trying to prevent Sophie from choosing Nathan, from choosing death. Stingo and Sophie are friends and eventually lovers; indeed, Sophie reveals more of her intimate and horrific past to Stingo than she does to her more dazzling lover, Nathan. Stingo screams "love me! Love life!" The problem is that his notion of life at twenty-two is far too innocent and naive to encompass a woman like Sophie.

Shortly before Stingo and Sophie flee the demonic Nathan, Stingo is invited to his friend Jack Brown's home in Nyack, New York, where he is promised sexual fulfillment with Jack's sister-in-law, Mary Alice Grimball. Mary is the opposite of Leslie in that she is prudish verbally but methodically masturbates Stingo without any pleasure; Stingo is not allowed to touch Mary Alice, describing his feelings as "lust and despair in almost equal measure." This insane activity prompts Stingo into his first homosexual dream, causing him to believe he "turned queer." Stingo feels imprisoned, unable to connect sexually, unsuccessful at his "lifelong efforts at good, wholesome, heterosexual screwing." Repression and sexual teasing leave Stingo wondering whether he is homosexual. While the dream reveals a strain of homophobia—if Stingo is not conquering women sexually he must be, lord forbid, "queer"—it also expresses Styron's real concerns about the suppression of healthy sexuality and its consequences.

While Stingo is detained by Mary Alice, the infamous "whack-off art-ist" in Nyack, Nathan is beating Sophie again in Brooklyn. Morris Fink calls Stingo in Nyack, so Stingo rushes back to Brooklyn to try to save Sophie. Since cohabitation is a sin according to the ethos of the times, Stingo knows that he will marry Sophie. It is at this point that Sophie realizes that her native Poland and Stingo's native America are both puritanical.

Stingo is further plagued by his Christian gentility in the hotel room he shares with Sophie in Washington. He has trouble getting aroused at first and feels ashamed when he touches her in her sleep. It is not until she initiates their paradisial lovemaking session in the middle of the night that Stingo can respond fully. For him it is the fulfillment of a potent fantasy. Stingo "feels the need to redefine joy, fulfillment, ecstasy, even God." This uninhibited initiation into the world of heterosexuality leaves him "verged on a scream, or a prayer." Finally, he experiences all he has read about or witnessed surreptitiously. This experience, ironically, is couched in religious terms—ecstasy, God, and prayer. Styron seems to be suggesting that the sexual act is both physical and spiritual, is as close to salvation as we humans are likely ever to get.

Although it is impossible for Sophie and Nathan and Sophie and Stingo, the older Stingo knows that love is the only bearable truth, that we must love all living things, a "fragile yet perdurable hope." After Stingo loses his two closest friends, he is grief stricken and brought to the brink of suicide. He goes back to Coney Island and is reminded of the "hollow lewdness" he experienced there by those suffering from "unearned unhappiness." These memories make Stingo want to drown; indeed, he dreams of being buried alive, yet he awakes to find himself surrounded by the sand some children covered him with to protect him through the night. Love is the only bearable truth, and sex is an important expression of our need to give and receive love. E. M. Forster's dictum, "Only connect," sums up the closing of the novel. The narrator argues that his thwarted passions did have a legitimate place in the narrative, and it has been amply demonstrated that his thwarted passions are more than just comic relief or inappropriate digressions; the emerging sexuality of Stingo and Sophie provides the symbolic setting in which the action of the novel can take solid form.

That their night of abandoned lovemaking means something quite different for Sophie is not due to their difference in gender but to their differences in age and personal experience, with Sophie's expression of her sexuality also at the core of this novel. Stingo says to Sophie in their Washington hotel room: "It's strange, mothers and fathers—they're at the core of one's own life somehow, or they can be." This intuition is crucial psychologically and thematically. It would be appropriate at this point to explore Sophie's sexuality as revealed throughout the narrative, its masochistic as well as its joyous elements, a joy which must be set against the more repressive and sexist attitudes of her time, a power which struggles, albeit unsuccessfully in her case, to assert the primacy of life over death, connectedness over isolation, individuality over mass conformity.

When we first meet Sophie in Brooklyn, she is deathly ill from her many months spent in Auschwitz. We are told that for months and even years she had no sexual cravings; survival was paramount. That is why Sophie herself is surprised when she gets sexually aroused while watching two lovers at Brooklyn College, the vision of them sparking her. Her dress at that time was generally quite conservative, "a psychic extension of the prudish way she cloaked herself in the rigid Catholic community of prewar Cracow." Generally, Sophie had a "guarded approach to sex." She tells Nathan there was no one but her husband in her life sexually and is reticent about revealing the digital rape to her boss, Blackstock. Sophie is described as a "young woman brought up with puritanical repressions and sexual taboos as adamantine as those of any Alabama Baptist maiden."

It was the morality of the time that dictated that Nathan and Sophie live apart, technically: they maintain two separate apartments although they are in effect living together. Yetta might have been broadminded enough to allow a tenant to entertain a male or female guest, but not so liberal as to allow an unmarried man and woman to live together. "This was still a time of worshipful wedlock and cold, marmoreal legitimacy and besides, it was Flatbush, a place as disposed to the extremes of propriety and to neighborly snooping as the most arrested small town in the American heartland." The older narrator links the puritanical morality of Catholic Poland, Baptist Alabama, and even Jewish Flatbush.

What then changes Sophie? The answer is Nathan. It is his unleashed sexuality which helps Sophie to unlock her buried eroticism; she even gets her sexual idiom from Nathan, freely spouting profanities, mimicking Nathan. Nathan and Sophie are verbally and literally sexually liberated, a stark contrast with Leslie Lapidus and Mary Alice Grimball and even Stingo himself, who is not only a virgin but unused to hearing profanities, especially when uttered by a woman. Nathan so helps to transform Sophie sexually that when she sees nuns in the neighborhood bar, Maple Court, she calls them, "silly, stupid virgins."

We discover that Sophie never loved her husband, Kazik, and that he and her lover, Jozef, were inhibited if not dysfunctional lovers. Sophie was sexually starved, but a woman of that generation never complained or demanded sexual gratification or equality. We are told she shared with her mother an "enforced obsequiousness." In Sophie's case, her father completely dominated her life even after she was married, and Sophie seems to have no conscious resentment of this tyranny. Her father says to her: "Your intelligence is pulp, like your mother's. I don't know where you get your body, but you did not get your brains from me." In short, Sophie's entire sense of self stemmed from her father, and when her father and husband are shot, Sophie's sense of self, her entire identity, becomes unfastened. Obviously, this will have dire consequences for her entire life; she will allow Nathan to have total control over her mind and body to the point where she feels she literally cannot and will not live without him. Nathan will continue where Sophie's father left off, verbally browbeating her, calling her every sexual epithet to demean her sense of worth. Here Styron reveals the global domination over women. It is not that women are inherently masochistic; rather, many have not known any other way to behave, never having had sufficient role models.

Sophie not only experienced a decidedly sexist and sexually repressed childhood and young adulthood, but she was also a victim of Auschwitz's special brand of sexual brutality. Sophie is nearly raped by a woman guard early in her stay at Auschwitz. Her sense of identity is so shaky she can barely remember her own name. We are informed that many guards were either prostitutes or lesbians. She is then raped by Wilhelmine, Höss's housekeeper. Höss himself denounces homosexuality, but his own sexuality is decidedly distorted. Höss's attitude towards women can be summed up as follows: "So few women have any informed knowledge or understanding about anything." What Höss does value, however, is female Aryan beauty, a beauty which he worships, prompting him to deposit his seed in these beautiful vessels. Sophie inspires in him this worship: sex at the service of political ideology. Curiously, Höss whispers to Sophie: "Having intercourse with you would allow me to lose myself; I might find forgetfulness." Sophie, too, will use sex at times to lose herself, to find forgetfulness. The irony here is that both Höss and Sophie feel like victims, needing escape and comfort. Sophie will find permanent forgetfulness through suicide, and Höss was hanged.

Another important pre-Brooklyn influence on Sophie is Wanda, a lesbian Resistance worker, courageous where Sophie is cowardly. Wanda is childless and so risks less than Sophie in defying the Third Reich. Styron seems to suggest here that Wanda, as a minority, can afford to be defiant because she is more disenfranchised with less to lose. The rebels in *Sophie's Choice* come from minority groups: Wanda, a lesbian, and Nathan, a Jew. Minority status is linked to moral superiority. Wanda is a wonderful woman who urges Sophie to use her sex for all its worth with Höss, who is just "another susceptible bureaucrat with a blocked-up itch for a female body." Sophie sleeps with Wanda once or twice, but she does not really respond to her "that way." Sophie says, "I loved her because she was better than me, and so incredibly brave." Lesbians, then, are not stereotyped; lesbian guards at Auschwitz victimize Sophie, but Wanda is portrayed as a totally admirable woman worthy of love, respect, and affection, an obvious rebuttal to Höss's generalization that all homosexuals are to be despised.

We also learn about Sophie's sexuality through her dreams. When Sophie is attracted to her father's acquaintance, the German industrialist Walter Dürrfeld, she guiltily thinks about going to early Mass the next day. In Auschwitz Sophie has a dream about Dürrfeld the night before she actually sees him in the camps—an example of precognition. In the dream, she is on a beach with a German man who strokes her buttocks and utters lewd words. They wander into a chapel, with Dürrfeld standing before an altar nude. He commands Sophie to perform fellatio, with Sophie nearly choking with pleasure. He then commands her to kneel at the altar while he penetrates her from behind. Obviously, this dream reveals Sophie's guilt over her supposed complicity with the Nazis. It also reveals her disillusionment with religion and with faith, as well as her need to be dominated sexually; clearly, there is an excitement involved in this degradation for her. We must keep in mind here that Sophie's husband was repelled by her body and that her lover, Jozef, was a young virgin. Sophie does love oral sex, but until she meets Nathan, she can experience it only in her dreams. Unfortunately, Sophie will act out the dream's sadism not with Dürrfeld in Auschwitz but with Nathan in Flatbush.

Another important dream Sophie has is a recurring one about listening to Princess Czartoryska playing Brahms. In the dream her father says, "Please don't play that music for the child. She is much too stupid to understand." Sophie intuits that in some way this meant that her father wanted her to die, since music was life itself for Sophie. This undoubtedly contributes to her low self-esteem and later to her masochistic sexuality and eventual suicide.

With Nathan she adopts a subservient stance; the one exception is her refusal to quit her job even though Nathan asks her to do so. She has a childlike dependence on him. When he leaves the room, Sophie feels as if she is being abandoned by her parents. She desires Nathan even when he is taunting or abusing her. During their fall foliage trip to Connecticut, Nathan kicks her, calls her Irma Griese, tries to urinate in her mouth, and kicks her ribs. While making oral love on the ground, Sophie's knees are gouged by shale, but she makes no move to ease the pain. Her greatest fear is that he will die and she will be the lone survivor again; for Sophie the pain of his torture is preferable to the nothingness of life without him. As Sophie says, "After all this I was still ready for Nathan to piss on me, rape me, stab me, beat me, blind me, do anything with me that he desired." But she continues, "fucking made me forget the pain but forget God too, and

Jan, all the other things I had lost." Nathan is correct when he calls Sophie almost "egoless." She herself knows that it was sick of her "to be just this little kitten for him to fondle. To fuck and fondle—." The narrator describes their sexuality as "despairing tenderness" and "perverse eroticism with its stink of death." Here, no doubt, Styron is linking the daily brutality in the camps with the sado-masochistic sexuality Sophie and Nathan engage in, a crucial link almost totally omitted in the film version of the novel.

An Italian film called *The Night Porter* by Liliana Cavani, made in 1974, did explore the relationship between the Nazis and sado-masochistic sexuality. The film examines the themes of guilt, incest, and the postwar legacy of the Holocaust. It is important to note here that the film was not American-made and garnered very mixed reviews in the United States. Some critics claimed the film exploited the Holocaust for the sake of sensationalism. Cavani, however, justified the depiction of brutal sexuality in a letter to *Le Monde:*

> Fascism is not only an event of yesterday. It is with us still, here and elsewhere. As dreams do, my film brings back to the surface a repressed 'history'; today this past is still deep within us. . . . What interested me was to explore this cellar of the present, to inquire into the human subconscious; it was to offer up that which troubles me in order to trouble others so that all of us can live wakefully. It was to stimulate, to give a point of departure for understanding why the fascists are again among us—not the old ones, the nostalgics who are, one might say, caricatures, but the new ones, the young antidemocrats of my generation. (Friedlander 129)

The movie depicts a young woman's slavish devotion to the Nazi who initiated her sexually in the camps. Her fascination for the Nazi extends beyond the camps; she and the ex-Nazi, Max, reunite in 1957 Austria and replay their concentration-camp scenes, showing how a powerful past locks them into the repetition compulsion. Max's guilt turns him into "a physically degraded and emotionally shattered prisoner" (Insdorf 116). They both become victims of their obsessive, brutal love, a mirror of their concentration-camp experience, and are consumed in death.

The perverse eroticism in *Sophie's Choice* is just as disturbing as that portrayed in *The Night Porter* and is meant to be. Styron, like Cavani, wants us to "live wakefully," to beware of the many hidden faces of fascism, for a refusal to look at this perversion can have serious consequences. The inclusion of sado-masochism in *The Night Porter* and *Sophie's Choice* is not for the sake of sensationalism, is not an exploitation of the Holocaust, but rather shows how our ignorance and naivete can only aid and abet brutality, political, sexual, or otherwise. Patterns of sexuality, then, are clearly historically and culturally determined.

We must also explore another important aspect of Sophie's sexuality:

the frank, liberated one. Sophie announces "I'm sexy" and indeed she is a mature woman, proud of her sexuality and sensuality. She is, as Styron calls her, "a superb woman," *woman* being the operative word here. With Nathan she shares a love of record albums, concerts, books, meals, wine, clothes, jewelry, and movies, in short, all the sensual pleasures. Both Nathan and Sophie had been sexually starved before their union. Nathan had known only Jewish American Princesses zealously guarding their virginity, and Sophie had an impotent husband and an inexperienced lover. Nathan, then, helps free Sophie from her guilt, especially her guilt about her strong desire for oral sex. Nathan buys Sophie a diaphragm, a symbolic token of her leave-taking from the church. Sophie says, "Never did I think two people could fuck so much. Or love it so much either." There is a sense, then, of Nathan's not only literally saving the emaciated Sophie but freeing her to be the kind of liberated sexual woman Catholic Poland had suppressed. Styron is obviously sympathetic with the need to bid farewell to Cracow's repressiveness and to defy American puritanism. When not marred by one of Nathan's mad frenzies, his lovemaking with Sophie is set up as a model of joyous, healthy sexuality, creative, individual, and free— something Stingo desperately desires for himself.

Sophie reveals her frank sexuality with Stingo as well, although her feelings for him are more friendly than amorous. On the beach Sophie reaches to touch Stingo "deep where thigh and buttock intersect." Stingo is taken aback by Sophie's unabashedly erotic gesture. Sophie also suggests they both undress at the beach. When she caresses him, Stingo ejaculates quickly, with Sophie responding that his ejaculation will be good for his complexion; she then proceeds to rub his semen into her face. We must remember here that her feelings for Stingo partly stem from the fact that he reminds her of Jozef, also an honest, direct, virginal young man. This scene is reminiscent of Robert Anderson's *Tea and Sympathy,* in which an older woman ministers to a younger, sexually insecure man—tenderly and sympathetically. In their last night together, Stingo is fully initiated into the world of "good, healthy, heterosexual screwing." We witness Sophie's "good, raw, natural animal passion," her expression so beautifully tender and drowned and abandoned in her passion that Stingo has to avert his gaze. At twenty-two, Stingo could not yet know that sex can sometimes be a flight from feeling. At that moment, Stingo's long-awaited experience of passionate, erotic lovemaking is only life affirming, not death defying.

What Styron makes clear in the novel, therefore, is that sex is rarely a life force; that repressions, perversions, and exploitations often prevent the natural expression of sexuality in modern civilization. Because of these culturally determined restraints, the sexual urge often expresses itself perversely, "masquerading as religious salvation ... or Freudian chic" (Ruder-

man 125), or in Höss's case, political ideology. *Sophie's Choice* demonstrates that real tenderness is a rarity in human relationships, that friendship
plays too small a role in our lives. The novel says a great deal about
unwanted solitude, about the difficulty of intimate connecting.

The novel is, after all, about the Holocaust, about the total breakdown
of the concept of brotherhood; the sexuality in it is therefore symbolic of
this breakdown, reminding us of what the Holocaust did and continues to
do to all of us. Without love and friendship, without intimate, tender connections, human beings often turn inward and sink into suicidal despair or
direct their emptiness and frustration outward and descend into homicidal
madness. Sophie is so tortured by her losses and by her very survival after
spending twenty months in Auschwitz herself that she chooses suicide;
Nathan is so affected imaginatively by the horrors of the Holocaust that
he too chooses suicide. Stingo is the lone survivor learning how to conquer
grief and despair so that he can go on living, the only character not destroyed by his suffering. Like Stingo, we must all come up cold against the
inferno while continuing our search for love, joy, and hope. We must all
seek "that essential region of the soul where absolute evil confronts brotherhood."

That search for love, joy, and hope is doomed to fail, however, if
individuals allow themselves to be subsumed into large groups, into repressive bureaucracies, like McGraw-Hill on a small scale and the Third Reich
on a larger, more treacherous one. Some claim love is doomed to fail
anyway after Auschwitz; indeed, we are all forced to reconsider how the
ravages of the Holocaust affect love and hope in the modern world. *Sophie's Choice,* urges us to retain some "fragile yet perdurable hope." Salvation, though, comes in the form of children protectively covering an adult
with sand, symbolically in moments of unselfish love, of instinctive identification with the plight of the suffering without which future Holocausts are
not only possible but probable.

4

Sophie's Choice:
An American Voyage into the Mystery of Iniquity

Styron, a Southerner by birth, was naturally influenced by the Southern literary tradition, particularly by the novels of Faulkner, Robert Penn Warren, and Thomas Wolfe; indeed, his first novel, *Lie Down in Darkness,* published in 1951, is heavily indebted to the themes and styles of Faulkner and Warren. Some critics hailed Styron in the early 1950s as the heir apparent to Faulkner's throne. These same critics, however, were disappointed by Styron's subsequent fiction because it was not "Southern enough," arguing that Styron had abandoned his true calling, his Southern roots. When asked if he considers himself part of a tradition of Southern writing, Styron responds he does not feel committed to the Southern tradition largely because the South has changed. Styron has been living in the North for over three decades, and while he acknowledges an attachment to and knowledge of the South, his non-Southern literary influences are formidable, including, among others, Shakespeare, Marlowe, Flaubert, Conrad, Joyce, Dostoevsky, Tolstoy, Melville, Fitzgerald, Camus, Malraux, Gide, Bellow, and Roth.

Despite this, some critics persist in pigeonholing Styron, particularly irksome because he is one of our least parochial novelists. Samuel Coale, author of several articles on Styron, calls *Sophie's Choice* a piece of "Southern Gothic fiction," in which the guilt is so overwhelming that attempts to transform it appear ludicrous and evasive. Coale concludes that feeling guilt is all there is in Styron's novel. To make matters worse, Coale insinuates that Styron is cowardly because his protagonists (here he is thinking of Nat Turner and Stingo) escape this nightmare vision all too easily, escape unscathed because the Gothic romance tradition does not embrace absolute evil, demanding the waking from the nightmare, a return to normality; Coale, therefore, sees Stingo's resurrection at the end of the novel as forced, a cowardly evasion. Styron, he told this writer, "avoids the contraries"; he insists that Styron is a "provisional rebel in Christian masquerade" (57).

Pauline Kael, the film critic for *The New Yorker*, calls *Sophie's Choice* Styron's "Holocaust Gothic" (74). She further asserts that the novel is all come-on, a striptease, sweetened along the way with "Gothic goodies like the Pink Palace" (75). The novel, for her, is garish and titillating, playing the readers for suckers.

What is important about these two assessments is not only that they are inaccurate, but that they obscure the meaning and importance of the novel, first by placing it in the wrong genre—Southern Gothic—and second by condemning the limitations of that genre. Styron's Pink Palace is light-years away from Faulkner's decaying mansions, from Gothic romance. To understand the symbolic structure and meaning of the novel we would be better served if we turned our attention away from the Southern literary tradition, as Styron urges us to do, to more solid and fertile ground, specifi-cally to two great symbolists: the nineteenth-century American novelist and poet Herman Melville and the twentieth-century French novelist and essay-ist Albert Camus; *Sophie's Choice* owes more to Melville and Camus than it does to the great "Dixie Special"—Faulkner. If we do not assess these influences, we cannot possibly appreciate the novel's architecture or under-stand the profound implications the novel has for contemporary readers. Let us begin with an exploration of the Melvillean overtones in *Sophie's Choice* and how these contribute to the novel's characters, action, and ideas, demonstrating that far from "avoiding the contraries," *Sophie's Choice* reveals the urgency and necessity of ramming right into them.

When asked in 1977, while writing *Sophie's Choice*, which novelists continue to mean the most to him, the first writer Styron mentioned was Melville. Already in the second paragraph of *Sophie's Choice* the reader is forced to make a connection with Melville since the paragraph begins with "Call me Stingo," echoing the famous beginning of *Moby-Dick*, "Call me Ishmael." Is this merely a rhetorical device? In a 1980 interview when asked why he chose to make the book partly autobiographical, Styron responded:

> I realized that this was very important in order to make this story as seductive as I could make it, as dramatically compelling. I had to back off and give the reader—from the very first page—a sense of who was talking, which is a very good dramatic device and an old-fashioned one, but one that if done properly almost never fails. It's at the heart of storytelling and is the art of the novel—to establish oneself with a great authority as the narrator who's going to tell you a very interesting story, but who has not gotten around to telling you the story yet. A good example of this device is *Moby-Dick* where Ishmael goes through a long, wonderfully comic episode in New Bedford right before he gets you on the ship. He establishes the right to dominate your attention. I didn't do this with anything so obvious as *Moby-Dick* for a model, but just used a device that has been used many, many times. (West 236)

Clearly, Stingo and Ishmael are youthful stand-ins for their creators. Both Melville and Styron strive for authority in their narrators; the fact that both narratives are told in the first person lends an intimacy and directness, and the fact that both narratives are told as reminiscences gives them greater richness. Beginning the novel with "Call me Stingo," therefore, is more than a safe rhetorical device. First, it tells us something about the character of the young, twenty-two-year-old narrator: that he is imaginative, literate, and a bit cocky. The tone is meant to be a bit mocking, comic. The name Stingo, after all, was derived from the nickname Stinky, referring to the narrator's hygiene. The beginning of the novel, then, is self-mocking, the older, more accomplished writer looking back at his younger, naive self. As such, *Sophie's Choice* is a *Künstlerroman,* a novel chronicling a writer's artistic development.

The implications of this link to Melville go much deeper than rhetorical strategies. It will be shown that *Moby-Dick* and *Sophie's Choice* share much in common in terms of their characters, ideas, themes, action, and overall architecture, that both novels are actually tragedies of madness and acts of metaphysical rebellion. Both Melville and Styron share Ishmael's view of mankind: "Heaven have mercy on us all—Presbyterians and Pagans alike—for we are all somehow dreadfully cracked about the head, and sadly need mending."

The first chapter of *Sophie's Choice* is reminiscent in many ways of the first chapter of *Moby-Dick,* entitled "Loomings." Both Stingo and Ishmael are young narrators with little or no money in their purses, without much stake in society, hostile to social institutions. They are both feeling a November in their souls. Stingo tells us that his youth at twenty-two "was at its lowest ebb." He could not produce a novel, he was out of work, had no money, and was a Southerner self-exiled in New York. It was, in short, a "morbid and solitary period." To keep the wolf from the door, Stingo becomes a reader for McGraw-Hill but feels a spiritual ache while working for this "soulless empire." Stingo is a lonely outcast, a "Southerner wandering amid the Kingdom of the Jews," suffering the "pain of unwanted solitude." Curiously, Stingo tells us he would like to be a writer someday with the soaring wings of a "Melville, Flaubert, or Tolstoy." To ease his solitude when not at work, Stingo tells us he is reading "The Bear," *Notes from the Underground,* and *Billy Budd;* that is, when he is not gazing out of his window consumed by sexual fantasies. Stingo is indeed "still very much feeling his oats." He knows enough at twenty-two, however, to know that he dislikes any "tidy, colorless and arch-conservative mold," and chafes at unthinking, mechanical, conforming men. Stingo refuses to wear a hat when ordered to and will not read the acceptable New York newspapers to conform to his boss's demands. Stingo is, then, an idealistic, ambitious youth on a spiritual quest, a rebellious voyager in search of the knowledge of good and evil, of knowledge of the self.

Stingo's view from the twentieth floor of his midtown office building gives him "spasms of exhilaration and sweet promise that have traditionally overcome provincial American youths." It is the Hudson he sees, and water imagery is important in this first chapter. We must remember that Stingo has just returned from the sea, having been a U.S. Marine in World War II, stationed in the South Pacific. Stingo sees a misty and obscure future when staring at the Hudson; his coworker Farrell stares often at the Hudson, his water gazing emblematic of terrible spiritual longing, having recently lost his son Eddie in Okinawa. When Stingo tells Farrell that he has been fired, Farrell responds, "People have been known to drown in this place." Stingo, normally a landsman, will be confronted by the destructive power of water but will also seek the purifying comfort of Coney Island after the deaths of his two closest friends.

We learn that Farrell sees Stingo as the promising writer his son can no longer be, whereas Stingo feels he has been deprived of something terrible and magnificent, having arrived in Okinawa after the shooting had ceased. Stingo muses on the incomprehensibility, the absurdity of time, of fate, which allowed Eddie to die in Okinawa while he, Stingo, was somehow spared what could have been that same fate. This realization causes him to conclude that all ambition is sad, that he carries a "large hollowness" within him, having been, until twenty-two at least, Fortune's darling. Stingo's self-assessment at the beginning of his voyage is this: "It was true that I had traveled great distances for one so young, but my spirit had remained landlocked, unacquainted with love and all but a stranger to death." Stingo knows he needs a "voyage of discovery," but little did he suspect at twenty-two that he would so quickly become acquainted with love and death in so strange a place to him as Brooklyn in 1947.

Ishmael, the isolato, experiences deep spiritual despair at the beginning of *Moby-Dick* and knows that he, too, must no longer remain landlocked. He takes to the sea to keep his madness under control, to "drive off the spleen and regulate the circulation," having been "involuntarily pausing before coffin warehouses and bringing up the rear of every funeral [he meets]." Ishmael in the insular city of the Manhattoes knows that the streets take you waterward, that thousands of men are "fixed in ocean reveries." "Meditation and water are wedded for ever." What unites men, Ishmael muses, is their need to get as close to the water as they can without falling in. We see ourselves in all rivers and oceans. "It is the image of the ungraspable phantom of life; and this is the key to it all." Ishmael, also normally a landsman, is a meditative, restless voyager needing to unlock his landlocked spirits. We could say, then, that *Sophie's Choice* and *Moby-Dick* are spiritual autobiographies, with Stingo and Ishmael the heroes who observe and participate during their voyages.

We also learn that Ishmael is like his creator in that they both were country schoolmasters, hailing from old established families and therefore unused to taking orders, yet he feels compelled to go on a whaling voyage, being ruled by "the invisible police officer of the Fates." Like Stingo, he is aware of the role of Fate in our destiny, aware that we are not entirely in control. While he does not understand fully at the beginning why the Fates have ordered him to go on this whaler, he knows it is somehow necessary to his development. Ishmael tells us that he is tormented with an everlasting itch for things remote. He "loves to sail forbidden seas and land on barbarous coasts." Both Stingo and Ishmael, then, establish themselves as lonely, sensitive, adventurous romantic questers in search of "things remote," knowing that they somehow must confront a "portentous and mysterious monster," not content with safe routines. Both leave their jobs to explore their souls. The opening chapters of both *Sophie's Choice* and *Moby-Dick*, therefore, are full of portentous loomings for the strange journeys that are to follow, metaphysical voyages into the mysteries of evil, madness, love, and death. Neither Stingo nor Ishmael ignores what is good, but Ishmael knows and Stingo will come to know how important it is "to perceive a horror" and "be social with it . . . since it is but well to be on friendly terms with all the inmates of the place one lodges in." Both Ishmael and Stingo discover that "unless you own the whale, you are but a provincial and sentimentalist in truth." Both will for a time be mesmerized by fatally glamorous heroes, Ahab and Nathan, will indeed identify with them.

It is not surprising, then, that Stingo is reading *Billy Budd* at the beginning of his journey or that he compares himself to Ishmael even mockingly or that one of Styron's and Stingo's favorite novelists is Melville. There are profound intellectual, emotional, and philosophical connections between Styron and Melville and, therefore, between Stingo and Ishmael, their youthful alter egos. The most profound similarity is their interest in metaphysical questions, their pondering the nature of being. Unsurprisingly, then, the problem of evil haunts both writers and spawns a moral quest, a search for values amid the stark realities of pain and suffering. Both writers stalk the riddles of personality and the riddles of existence, dramatizing human tensions without necessarily resolving them neatly. It is much easier for a twentieth-century novelist to do this than it was for Melville, who met a hostile response with the publication of *Moby-Dick*.

Why did he meet with such hostility during his lifetime? The overwhelming answer is that Melville was out of step with the prevailing mood of mid-nineteenth-century America, which was optimistic, expansionistic, and still terribly naive, an America that had won the War of 1812 and had more recently won the Mexican War, an overconfident, young America. It was an America that believed itself the chosen land, destined for some future unrelated to the vast flux of history, the city on the hill, a beacon of hope, an alternative to European Machiavellianism. The prevailing philosophy to match those soaring spirits was Transcendentalism, a belief in the goodness of the universe and God, a belief in the emblematic nature of the universe in which nature and spirit are one. Transcendentalism searched for reality through spiritual intuition. In short, it was a visionary, idealistic philosophy which held that human beings are related to all nature; they are not aliens. Its leading proponents were, of course, Emerson, Thoreau, and Whitman—three rugged individualists who believed wholeheartedly in this new democratic experiment, who believed that evil was merely the privation of good, that people were at peace with their environment since matter and spirit were one, that divinity lay in all living things, a primitive Pantheism; thus, Emerson could write the following in his journal during the middle of the Civil War, November 1863:

> We, in the midst of a great Revolution, still enacting the sentiment of the Puritans, and the dreams of young people thirty years ago; we, passing out of the old remainders of barbarism into pure Christianity and humanity, into freedom of thought, of religion, of speech, of the press, and of trade, and of suffrage, or political right; and working through this tremendous ordeal, which elsewhere went by beheadings, and massacre, and reigns of terror,—passing through all this and through states and territories, like a sleep, and drinking our tea the while. 'Tis like a brick house moved from its old foundations and place, and passing through our streets, whilst all the family are pursuing their domestic work inside. (Whicher 399)

Melville, however, could not subscribe to this view, nor could his friend and neighbor Hawthorne. The two writers launched an all-out attack on such dangerous naivete, their writing revealing their passionate conviction about the omnipresent existence of evil in human beings and nature, and their deep belief that such innocence was not only naive but potentially dangerous. Melville saw good and evil as independent forces at war for control, closer to Zoroastrianism or Manicheism, courageously rebuking the prevailing empty optimism in American thought, viewing man as a stranger, an orphan, exiled and abandoned in dangerous waters.

Such an insistence on man's darker side had its consequences and still does today. Styron, too, insists that we look at our darker selves, our potential for evil and destruction; if we neglect to do so, we are doomed. In twentieth-century America, however, pessimism is an easy commodity, this century having been particularly barbaric. While Americans can argue that Auschwitz was a European phenomenon, Styron knows that Americans cannot claim innocence; in 1979, when *Sophie's Choice* was published, America had just withdrawn its forces from the undeclared, bloody, protracted war in Vietnam. The older Stingo knows this when telling his story of Nazi horrors, horrors which did not end with the fall of the Third Reich. The younger narrator knows nothing about the concentration camps at the beginning of his journey, but by the end he can no longer claim ignorance as an excuse. Morris Fink's 1947 question, "What's Oswitch?" would no longer be acceptable since such ignorance is fatal. Styron, too, pays for his beliefs; he is appreciated much more in Europe than in this country precisely because he is candid in his criticism of American innocence and naivete and insistent about our necessity to experience evil within us, a potentially liberating experience. He demonstrates that Americans are not chosen people, just painfully ignorant of history and, therefore, overly optimistic. Some critics called Styron's second novel, *Set This House on Fire*, more French than American, and Styron himself calls France his spiritual home. Essentially, Styron's vision is more European, more Manichean, more aware of our duality. *Sophie's Choice* reflects this European outlook. In 1984, Styron was awarded the medal of the Commander of the Legion of Honor for his work, the highest honor the French government bestows; in France *Sophie's Choice* is considered one of the most significant novels to have emerged since World War II.

Melville had to obscure his real meanings in *Moby-Dick* and his subsequent fiction to make it more palatable for his readers. Styron does not use disguises, and has been heavily criticized during the last twenty years for his unflinching portrait of slavery in America in *The Confessions of Nat Turner* and his portrait of anti-Semitism, sexism, and racism in *Sophie's Choice*. The mystery of iniquity does indeed haunt Melville and Styron, permeating their fiction and their tragic view of human existence. Styron explained why Americans balk at this viewpoint in a 1962 interview in France for *L'Express*, right after *Set This House on Fire* was published to great acclaim in France but met with a lukewarm response in America:

> American society is an overly optimistic society. Except for the Civil War, it has never known tragedy and horror on its own soil. . . . It is more difficult for America than for Europe to conceive of tragedy. Americans do not like being told that people can be unbalanced, desperate, sometimes corrupt, that life can be horrible. . . . And they reject any tragic representation of life, not realizing that this representation can be a catharsis, that to accept a tragic picture of life on the artistic level can indeed free one from the horror so that one may enjoy life more. (West 24)

Obviously, then, Melville and Styron share an important philosophical way of perceiving the world and human nature, a view acutely aware of human history and our potential, a view which is difficult and at times dispiriting but also potentially freeing. Both Melville and Styron, at least the Melville of *Moby-Dick,* provide a way out of future barbarisms, a way towards the regeneration of our souls. It is a humanistic, not a religious resurrection, however, a vision of brotherhood as our only salvation, a vision which shapes the artistic endings of *Moby-Dick* and *Sophie's Choice.*

Melville and Styron also share a curious personal history regarding slavery, which prompts them to address questions of racial divisiveness in their fictions. We must not forget that *Moby-Dick,* published in 1851, was written in a time of great national crisis over the slave question. Slavery was the dominant issue being debated in 1850, and Melville and others feared the slavery issue would tear the Union apart—which, of course, it did just a short decade after *Moby-Dick* was published.

Melville was not just abstractly aware of the slavery crisis; his own father-in-law, Judge Lemuel Shaw, was the first Northern judge to enforce a rigorous 1850 fugitive slave law providing for interstate extradition for escaped slaves and heavily penalizing anyone aiding fugitive slaves. He ordered the return of runaway slave Thomas Sims to his master. Judge Shaw also upheld the Boston Primary School Committee's right to enforce segregated schooling, which was to establish a basis for the separate but equal doctrine. We could speculate that Melville harbored tremendous guilt about his family's close connection to promoting slavery, especially since Lemuel Shaw often supported Melville financially. It is not surprising, then, that race figures prominently in Melville's fiction. Melville understood that slavery deforms its victims and victimizers, generating an endless cycle of vengeance, a theme explored fully in his 1856 novella, *Benito Cereno.* The Civil War, as Melville predicted in *Moby-Dick,* would engulf all Americans, guilty and innocent, white and black, Northern and Southern.

Like Melville, Styron has a close personal link with slavery. Recently, Styron wrote a tribute to his late friend, writer James Baldwin, acknowledging that Baldwin's "soul's savage distress" helped shape and define his own work and its moral contours. Styron muses, "this would be the most appropriate gift imaginable to the grandson of a slave owner from a slave's grandson" ("Jimmy in the House"). Styron's paternal grandmother, Marianna Clark, born in 1848, owned two small black handmaidens throughout the Civil War. This tainted inheritance shows up fictionally in the guise of Artiste, a slave child the sale of whom provides Stingo with a small income which enables him to continue writing. Although Stingo is desperate for money at twenty-two while trying to write his first novel, he is nevertheless secretly happy when his apartment is burglarized and Artiste's money is stolen.

Also linking Styron with slavery is the place he grew up: Southampton

County, Virginia, the same county in which Nat Turner led his slave revolt. Styron knew when quite young that he would one day write about this remarkable man. In 1967, he published *The Confessions of Nat Turner,* engendering a Pulitzer Prize and a good deal of hostility from black readers and from critics who accused him of being a racist. Styron's ambivalence towards the South appears in some of his fiction, as in Stingo's occasional yearning for the old bucolic South in contrast with the reality of the new, industrially blighted South. Styron feels compelled to tackle the stain of slavery in his fiction and nonfiction. Curiously, Melville and Styron are white writers who have written fictions about slave rebellions from the slave's point of view, trying to understand the victims and the victimizers of this tragedy, perhaps exorcising some of their own sense of shame. Styron is aware that his *Confessions of Nat Turner* is part of a tradition in American literature based on an awareness of racial division. He expanded on this in a 1968 interview shortly after his novel was published:

> I think the *Confessions* is just a continuation of a tradition which we're going to find more and more of. An important strand of American literature is based on a consciousness of this division in our culture, this racial division. Melville had it; Mark Twain had it; Faulkner certainly had it; Sherwood Anderson had it; and Richard Wright had it. To some extent, it's been a large, important stream in the Mississippi River of our literature. I think that my book will have its place as part of this consciousness that we all share, black and white. Ralph Ellison's next novel, which has been a long time in preparation, shows a daring boldness on his part to penetrate into the white consciousness. Without such efforts, I visualize an America where we will not be able to exist unless we exist together. I fully believe this; I don't believe we can exist apart. The awareness of this, I think, will only come through literature which allows both black and white to courageously venture into each other's consciousness. I think it's a denial of humanity, of our mutual humanity, to assume that it is pretentious and arrogant and wrong for a white man to attempt to get into a black man's skin. (West 103–4)

What is important about this biographical information is that *Moby-Dick* and *Sophie's Choice* are not obviously about slavery, but if we investigate more closely, slavery—that is, the propensity for human beings to dominate others—is a crucial theme in both novels. Both novels are cautionary tales about this evil propensity and how a society may not allow this domination without being at risk of moral and physical collapse. Symbolically, the destruction of the *Pequod* suggests the destruction of the Union. Ahab ultimately rejects Pip; Stubb demeans Fleece and abandons Pip to the pitiless ocean. The harmony that does remain is Queequeg's friendship with Ishmael, suggesting that interracial harmony is not just an admirable, abstract ideal but a necessity for human survival. Similarly, in *Sophie's Choice*, Stingo understands that he must not profit from the sale of the slave Artiste. More importantly, Stingo learns that hatred of a race or ethnic group leads to Auschwitz. The older Stingo explains that Auschwitz was a system based on the view that life is totally expendable.

Sophie's Choice links, then, the two horrors of modern times—slavery and genocide in the American South, and slavery and genocide in Nazi Eastern Europe, demonstrating that Auschwitz was a part of a long history of global slavery, unique, though, because of the added concept of the absolute superfluity of human life which authorized mass extermination; Styron, therefore, draws a daring parallel between the Old South and Nazism. In this sense, *Sophie's Choice* can be read as a continuation of *The Confessions of Nat Turner*.

Essentially, Melville and Styron both subscribe to Melville's dictum: "To write a mighty book you need a mighty theme." Both writers are aware of the sinister forces in history and modern life which threaten all of humanity, thus giving their fictions larger tragic dimensions. Melville and Styron share an existential vision, urging that we must search for faith and certitude, for values, in a pandemonious world symbolized by bondage and oppression, a world hostile or at best indifferent to our needs. We must, then, always be in spiritual revolt against the evil and chaos in the universe.

This brings us to Ahab and his connection to *Sophie's Choice*. There were mythic fictional heroes in revolt before Ahab. We think automatically of Prometheus, who challenged Zeus's authority, the Satanic Hero, cast out of heaven by Michael, and the romantic Byronic hero. Certainly, Melville had these heroes in mind as well as the biblical wicked King Ahab, slavemaster and worshiper of false idols, when he created Ahab. While Ahab is an admirable character in many ways, rebuking life for its incompleteness because of death and its wastefulness because of evil, he is also terribly dangerous to himself and others. Melville points out the limits of the Byronic and Satanic heroes, heroes whose strong will to power can lead to narcissism and despotism. His portrait of Ahab also rebukes his contemporaries, Emerson and Carlyle, by dramatizing the dangers of blind hero worship and total self-reliance. In 1837 Emerson read Carlyle's review of the *Mémoires* of the French Revolution's statesman Mirabeau and noted in his journal:

> Then he is a worshipper of strength, heedless much whether its present phase be divine or diabolic. Burns, George Fox, Luther, and those unclean beasts Diderot, Danton, Mirabeau, whose sinews are their own and who trample on the tutoring and conventions of society, he loves. For he believes that every noble nature was made by God, and contains, if savage passions, also fit checks and grand impulses within it, hath its own resources, and however erring, will return from far. (Whicher 61)

Shortly thereafter, Emerson wrote his famous essay "Self-Reliance," a manifesto urging us to believe in the dignity and sanctity of the self, in individualism above all else. Transcendentalism encouraged what we now call charisma. A few quotations from his essay give the flavor of his manifesto:

> To believe your own thoughts, to believe that what is true for you in your private heart is true for all men,—that is genius. Speak your latent conviction, and it shall be the universal sense. (Whicher 147)

> Whoso would be a man, must be a nonconformist. He who would gather immortal palms must not be hindered by the name of goodness, but must explore if it be goodness. Nothing is at least sacred but the integrity of your own mind. Absolve you to yourself, and you shall have the suffrage of the world. (Whicher 149)

> No law can be sacred to me but that of my nature. Good and bad are but names very readily transferable to that or this; the only right is what is after my constitution; the only wrong what is against it. A man is to carry himself in the presence of all opposition as if every thing were titular and ephemeral but he. (Whicher 150)

> What I must do is all that concerns me, not what the people think. This rule, equally arduous in actual and in intellectual life, may serve for the whole distinction between greatness and meanness. It is the harder because you will always find those who think they know what is your duty better than you know it. It is easy in the world to live after the world's opinion; it is easy in solitude to live after our own; but the great man is he who in the midst of the crowd keeps with perfect sweetness the independence of solitude. (Whicher 151)

> And truly it demands something godlike in him who has cast off the common motives of humanity and has ventured to trust himself for a taskmaster. High be his heart, faithful his will, clear his sight, that he may in good earnest be doctrine, society, law, to himself, that a simple purpose may be to him as iron necessity is to others! (Whicher 161)

Does this not sound like Ahab—"And it truly demands something godlike in him who has cast off the common motives of humanity and has ventured to trust himself for a taskmaster"? We can view the portrait of Ahab as Melville's answer to Emerson and Carlyle. As such, *Moby-Dick* is a Transcendental parody. Ahab is the incarnation of the self-reliance doctrine gone mad. What Melville wants us to see is that strong leaders, strong individuals, do not have to be great ones; they can be selfish and destructive by casting off the common motives of humanity, such as survival and brotherhood. Ahab demands to be recognized as a distinct personality in the midst of the personified impersonal, and we admire his ability to assert his individualism; however, Ahab is essentially tyrannical and manipulative, with a will to power that will cause the destruction of the *Pequod* and its thirty isolatoes, exclusive of Ishmael. Ahab is grand but also fatally glamorous. While we admire his rebelliousness, his ability to feel profound outrage at life's injustices, we must also be frightened and outraged by his shameful recklessness, his disregard for human life, his evil. In short, Ahab is the era's "most fully developed oxymoronic character, attaining a kind of universality from the magnitude of the contrary impulses he embodies." (Reynolds 157)

It is not surprising that *Moby-Dick* has greater appeal for twentieth-century readers than for nineteenth-century readers. In 1887, only 4,000 copies of *Moby-Dick* were printed and sold. There were heavy sales, however, from 1921 to 1947. Our century responds to Melville's restless, puzzled, questioning spirit, to his intuitive understanding of the power of the unconscious, of the primitive within us. Melville understood there was no resolving the tensions between Transcendentalism and Empiricism, between religion and science, faith and skepticism; his spirit is essentially modern: alienated, divided, skeptical.

Melville scholars are reinterpreting Melville in light of feminism, Freud, the proletariat, Eros, and Nazi Germany. There has even been an argument advanced that *Moby-Dick* is a novel of political prophecy; that is, Melville's portrait of the charismatic yet tyrannical Ahab prefigures twentieth-century fascism. It is in this regard that *Moby-Dick* has eerie parallels in *Sophie's Choice*. Christopher S. Durer has written a provocative piece originally presented before the Melville Society in the summer of 1986 entitled "*Moby-Dick* and Nazi Germany." Durer begins his essay by acknowledging the recent interest in the political world of Melville's writings, making us more aware of Melville's stature as a liberal thinker and of the political and economic tensions which shaped his writing. This new political criticism, which began in the 1960s and has grown stronger in the 1980s, sees *Moby-Dick* as

> growing out of the aftermath of the Mexican War, with its rabid political and economic expansionism, the burning issue of the treatment of the Indians, and the apparently insoluable problem of slavery. The interregional and interracial society on board the *Pequod*, the structure of power which she exhibits, and numerous political allusions establish her as the ship of state in mid-nineteenth-century America. (Durer 1)

Durer takes this political criticism one step further by arguing that *Moby-Dick* is a book of political prophecy, "this time pointing to the inhumanities of twentieth-century totalitarianism, especially the National Socialist regime in Germany between 1933 and 1945" (Durer 1). He develops this analogy in two ways: first, by describing Ahab's propagandistic techniques, similar to those used in Nazi Germany, and second, by exploring Melville's understanding of the "very psychology and psychosis of power in a totalitarian state, such as Nazi Germany" (2). For Durer, then, *Moby-Dick* anticipates, psychologically and politically, the tragedies of our century. It "projects a macabre vision of twentieth-century fascism and offers a schema and typology of this fascism—its precarious beginnings, its growth and zenith, its death rattle, and its demise" (Durer 4). Durer shows how demagogues begin with limited powers and then obtain greater dominion by fomenting fear and hatred. Like Hitler, Ahab reaches for the "folk-soul" of the crew and manipulates their minds with sinister skill. A charismatic leader can tap and redirect primitive hatreds and racial animosities. Here is Melville's description of the *Pequod* crew under Ahab's rule: "Like machines, they dumbly moved about the deck, ever conscious that the old man's despot eye was on them." "They were one man, not thirty . . . and were all directed to that fatal goal which Ahab their one Lord and keel did point to."

Again, paralleling the transformation of the German nation under the Nazis, the crew of the *Pequod* becomes "a folk organism and not an economic organization," (Durer 9) since Ahab rejects the commercial benefits of whaling for a collective psychological fulfillment, resulting from the revengeful pursuit of one whale, seen as the enemy of the state. The mystique Ahab creates for himself is similar to Hitler's psychological enslavement of the German nation and his notion of himself as the leader; consequently, rather than being a type of pre-twentieth-century absolute ruler, Ahab is in reality a prototype of a twentieth-century fascist dictator, someone like Adolf Hitler. *Moby-Dick,* according to Durer, is both a cry of anguish and a dark historical prophecy.

Essentially, Durer demonstrates that ideology deadens and depersonalizes; human beings become robots, resulting from a particular political ethos. The crew functions like a machine, with lifeless obedience amounting to political automatism. Captain Ahab identifies the white whale as the enemy of the state, a threat to the collective will; Moby Dick, however, is merely an archetypal victim on whose hump Ahab piles "the sum of all the general rage and hate felt by his whole race from Adam down." To preserve its monolithic character, a group needs an enemy that gives it security and cohesion. Melville presents to us those who would be susceptible to excessive authority—mongrel renegades, castaways, and cannibals—the dispossessed and the violence-oriented; therefore, *Moby-Dick* depicts the soil in which fascism can flourish. There can be no redemption or self-fulfillment in obedience; the crew must share some of the guilt for the destruction of the *Pequod,* for their own destruction. This kind of evil defies rational solutions. Interestingly, Ahab and Hitler end up as suicides when their empires collapse. Mythic heroes are usually rehabilitated or redeemed, but there can be no redemption for Ahab. We need Ishmael's recounting of this tragic story so that we might be redeemed. Durer sums up the importance of *Moby-Dick* as follows:

> *Moby-Dick* portrays deep subterranean social forces—the different dynamics of society, the psychologies of the crowd, ruthless pursuits of power, the frailties of social organisms under pressure—all of which pose monumental problems and ultimately defy solutions, pointing at the same time to the catastrophies and cataclysms of the twentieth century. (Durer 12)

We must remember that every ship was, in those days, a tyranny; nevertheless, Ahab's story has profound social and political implications, not only for America in 1850 but also for twentieth-century readers. The connection to *Sophie's Choice* is both obvious and subtle; Ahab is a proto-type for twentieth-century dictators, for the Third Reich we confront in *Sophie's Choice,* but he also resembles one of the three main characters in the novel—Nathan. The biblical Ahab was a wicked king, but the biblical Nathan was the prophet who rebuked King David for his murder of Uriah. We are meant, therefore, to conceive of Nathan as a moral exemplar, and, in some ways, Nathan is quite literally a gift to humanity as his name suggests; however, Nathan, like Ahab, like Hitler, is determined to rid the world of what he considers to be evil, to fight evil with evil. Ahab wanted to destroy Moby Dick and thereby cleanse the world of malice. Hitler wanted to rid the world of undesirables—Jews, homosexuals, Slavs, Gyp-sies, Poles, the handicapped—to create a purified Aryan race. Nathan wants to destroy the evil the Holocaust represents, wants to rid the world of torturers, tyrants, anti-Semites, and collaborators, as his battering of Sophie indicates. The profound connection between Ahab and Nathan is that they both see the overwhelming malice in the universe and feel outraged by its power and capriciousness; they understand that our highest goal is to strike through the mask. They do not, however, stop at feeling outraged by life's injustices and cruelties. Both Nathan and Ahab incorporate the evil into themselves, use the "enemy's" methods; that is, they are dependent some-what on the evil and their spiritual revolts take on a murderous edge.

Though outraged by life's cruelties represented by the inscrutable and ubiquitous whale, Ahab becomes capricious and cruel himself, forsaking human fellowship for diabolical ends. We might contrast here Ahab's reac-tion to the loss of his leg with the response of Jack Brown, Stingo's friend, who lost his leg during the Second World War. Jack Brown had a "mad and sovereign stoicism that prevented him from falling into suicidal despair." Ironically, the artificial leg which replaces the one torn off Ahab by Moby

Dick is made of whale jawbone, so that Ahab's mobility is literally owed to a dead whale. Though Starbuck, Pip, and other ships' captains warn him of the folly and futility of his chase, Ahab will not swerve from his ill-fated course; he has fallen into the abyss. Still, Melville wants us to feel that Ahab's clever villainy is preferable to society's established hypocrisy.

Nathan, like his biblical namesake, takes a strong stand against murder but ultimately becomes evil himself. We must remember, of course, that Nathan is quite literally mad. Diagnosed as a paranoid schizophrenic, he has been in and out of mental institutions for much of his life; his is not a rational mind, whereas the appalling nature of Ahab's and Hitler's crimes was indeed their incredible rationality, their deliberateness, their efficiency. Nathan's crimes are irrational, his attacks on Sophie often induced by drugs or madness, his fits of jealousy and violence sudden, unplanned, impulsive. We must remember that Nathan fears genocide in this country, becoming increasingly enraged when he hears about the camps, the Nuremburg trials, and Göring's suicide. The awful, bitter irony, however, is that Nathan, who rages against the Nazis' use of cyanide gas to destroy millions of Jews, swallows a cyanide tablet to kill himself, uses, in effect, the Nazis' methods, their technology of death; Nazi evil, therefore, becomes his evil. Psychologically, some have described this phenomenon as a victim's identification with his victimizer, which creates a horrible chain of compulsive behavior affecting generations. Both Ahab and Nathan would have done well to read Augustine's *Confessions:* "I sought whence is evil; and sought it in an evil way; and saw not the evil in my very search."

Part of the power of *Sophie's Choice,* then, lies in its dramatization of what the Holocaust has done to a generation of people, Americans and Europeans, and how it continues to cause anguish, pain, unforgettable evil, and torment. We see what the Holocaust has literally done to Sophie and what it imaginatively has done to Nathan, whose schizophrenia represents the world's wounds, and we see how the innocent Stingo learns about the unspeakable horror through his love for Sophie and friendship with Nathan. All this adds up to a rich texture of horror, and as readers we respond to the novel as we would a Greek tragedy, with awe, pity, and fear.

Both *Moby-Dick* and *Sophie's Choice* dramatize how all of us are enveloped in whale-lines, how we all walk into the jaws of the whale; it is the human condition. There is no comfortable wisdom, and this truth makes us sorrowful. Melville tells us that the truest of all men was Solomon, the Man of Sorrows, who despaired of solving the mystery of the universe; Stingo prefers to read Ecclesiastes and Isaiah, not the Sermon on the Mount, because Hebrew woe seemed more cathartic. Styron, like Melville, sees the value in suffering, indeed sees suffering as a moral quality that can drive human beings to self-understanding and give them the chance of purification and transformation, leading them to freedom and human dignity, symbolized by Melville's Catskill eagle in "The Try-Works" chapter.

Too much sorrow, however, is destructive. Ahab has "his humanities" but will ultimately abandon his kindred spirit, Pip. Nathan is most attracted to Flaubert's *Madame Bovary* because of Emma's suicidal resolution and sees suicide as the legitimate option of any sane human being after the Third Reich. Stingo and Ishmael, however, after coming as close to the water's edge of despair as is humanly possible, learn how to conquer their grief. This is not to say that the two narrators are no longer sorrowful men, for they are, but they have earned their unhappiness and gain dignity and strength from their short stay in the abyss. The Greeks understood that there is no wisdom without suffering. Both Ishmael and Stingo, and Melville and Styron by extension, urge us towards this hard-earned wisdom, towards the wisdom that is woe, an uncharacteristically American view.

What happens, however, when that woeful wisdom becomes intolerable? Ahab's murderous monomania and Nathan's suicidal schizophrenia are obvious results. But there are two characters less obviously devastated by wisdom, one minor, one major: Pip in *Moby-Dick* and Sophie. Both Pip and Sophie are dealt blows which they are incapable of surviving: theirs is the woe that is madness, both victims of life's wantonness. Pip is the black cabin boy whose tambourine music uplifts the *Pequod's* crew. Superficially, Pip appears to be the stereotypically happy, music-loving slave. Actually, Pip is closer to Lear's wise fool, warning against folly. Pip is stung by life's injustices, but his passive response is in direct contrast with Ahab's vengeful protests. Pip's madness is acquiescence. Pip has been thrown overboard to the sharks symbolically. Hours later, by chance, not design, Pip is rescued by the *Pequod,* but by this time he has, it seems, lost his mind. This crucial chapter in *Moby-Dick,* called "The Castaway," dramatizes most graphically the narrator's feelings that the universe is a "heartless immensity." Ishmael hints that Pip's madness is caused by the fact that the sea carried him

> down alive to wondrous depths, where strange shapes of the unwarped primal world glided to and fro before his passive eyes; and the miser-merman, Wisdom, revealed his hoarded heaps; and among the joyous, heartless, ever-juvenile eternities, Pip saw the multitudinous, God-omnipresent, coral insects, that out of the firmament of waters heaved the colossal orbs. He saw God's foot upon the treadle of the loom, and spoke it; and therefore, his shipmates called him mad. So man's insanity is heaven's sense; and wandering from all mortal reason, man comes at last to that celestial thought, which, to reason, is absurd and frantic; and weal or woe, feels then uncompromised, indifferent as his God. (Melville 599)

The universe, Ishmael suggests, is absurd, frantic, indifferent, a realization too overwhelming for some. True wisdom—that is, an accurate perception of God's malice—is maddening. Ahab's response is to strike through the pasteboard mask of appearances. But how many would want to strike through the mask if on the other side were nothing? Pip's madness is terror, and is less noble than defiance, but is still superior to "right reason." If the universe is indifferent, it is wise to celebrate the value of human friendship, of love. At weak moments, Ahab almost abandons his maniacal course when he allows himself to identify with Pip's suffering, to empathize with other human beings. Pip shows us the importance of human solidarity in a universe in which human beings are strangers, aliens, the pitiful waste of Ahab's antisocial, antilife behavior. An essential question *Moby-Dick* poses, then, is how can the innocent, symbolized here by Pip, protect themselves from the sharks without adopting evil methods themselves. The answer suggested is by going mad and not by doing evil. This question has profound importance for the twentieth century and brings us to Sophie Zawistowska.

Sophie, as her name suggests, is wise; she has fully experienced life's sharkishness. Sophie, more than most, has been forced to stare into the face of evil and not only come up cold against the inferno but live in it, forced to make infernal choices. How is one to survive such "wisdom"? What *Sophie's Choice* dramatizes is that no one can stare into the face of evil that long and survive. Sophie physically survives her twenty months in Auschwitz, but it is clear from the beginning of the novel that part of Sophie is already dead, and the remaining part longs for total annihilation. One of the most profound implications of *Sophie's Choice* is that survivors of the Holocaust can never totally recover, can possibly survive physically but not emotionally or spiritually. While psychologists give this condition a name—post-traumatic shock syndrome—the truth is that Sophie's "illness" is more than a syndrome, more than shock waves following the experience of war. Both *Moby-Dick* and *Sophie's Choice* urge us to acknowledge cosmic evil and the shark within, to be curious about and familiar with it. Dwelling on the horrors of existence, however, will produce madness, which can take a passive form, as in the cases of Pip and Sophie, or a very active form, as in the cases of Ahab and Nathan.

Sophie begs Nathan to abandon his mad quest, which is seemingly a quest to destroy Sophie but is actually a quest to destroy evil. Sophie, to Nathan, is a living reminder of all those who died in the concentration camps, his pain exacerbated by the fact that she is a Gentile survivor. In striking Sophie, Nathan is attempting to harpoon his own Moby Dick, the incarnation of the world's evil. Sophie, he feels, is a Nazi collaborator and is, therefore, a Nazi herself. At first, Nathan views Sophie as the unfortunate victim of a horrific era and nurtures her lovingly back to health. Anytime Nathan reads or hears about the camps or the SS, however, he takes out his rage against Sophie, who metaphorically has stolen a piece of Nathan: she lives while Nathan's "Jewish brothers" have perished. We must remember, of course, that Nathan is a schizophrenic and drug addict and represents the world's wounds. There is no way, then, for Sophie to deter Nathan, a fact which ultimately leads to her own destruction as well. Pip, too, is destroyed because he cannot deter Ahab from his course. The difference is that Pip is killed along with the other crew members when Moby Dick proves mightier than Ahab, but Sophie chooses to die. She can neither live with nor live without Nathan; he is merely her final torturer. Like Pip, Sophie can never really recover from life's blows anyhow, from the accuracy of her perception of the world's malice. Stingo is right when he says that Sophie would be able to endure any hell in the afterlife.

Sophie had attempted suicide right after the liberation of Auschwitz and flirted with it during a weekend in Connecticut with Nathan where he dangled a cyanide capsule in front of her mouth; she also tried to drown herself at Coney Island and was rescued by the innocent Stingo, determined to save her at any cost. Sophie, however, had seen the heartless immensity of the universe; the infinite of her soul had been drowned long before the actual suicide. Sophie saw the indifference of nature, of God, and knew that God was dead; either he abandoned her or she abandoned him. She did not have the ability to revolt against the chaos and evil in the universe; having been too maimed by the inferno, she was no longer able to believe in a future. Through Sophie, Stingo experiences the inferno firsthand and begins to recognize the appalling enigma of human existence. Like all of us, Stingo is forced to consider whether Auschwitz was "a fatal embolism in the bloodstream of mankind." Is loving an absurdity after Auschwitz? Interestingly, *Moby-Dick* asks a similar question a century before the Holocaust: Are friendship and love possible in a sharkish world? The answer is a fragile yet real half-blind yes.

The other curious similarity between Pip and Sophie is the fact that they are slaves of sorts, Pip because of his color in mid-nineteenth-century America, and Sophie because she is Polish in Europe in the 1940s. Both love music and are capable of feeling and expressing ecstasy, yet Pip and Sophie are both considered commodities, both incarnations of the two horrors of modern times—slavery and genocide in America, and slavery and genocide in Nazi Eastern Europe, two victims of racial madness, of bigotry, of systems that dare to think of themselves as "brotherly," as paternal. Stubb orders Fleece to serve him and abandons Pip to the vast ocean. Dürrfeld, the German industrialist, says to Höss: "I am answerable to a corporate authority which is now simply insisting on one thing: that I be supplied with more Jews in order to maintain a predetermined rate of production.... We must have the coal.... I must have more Jews." Both

Melville and Styron provide alternatives to authoritarian "brotherhood," to systems which degrade and demean the dignity of human life, to systems which "commodify" human beings.

The links between Ishmael and Stingo, Ahab and Nathan, and Pip and Sophie have been demonstrated. The obvious character excluded is the whale itself—Ahab's powerful antagonist—with its parallel in *Sophie's Choice*—the Holocaust. A little more than a quarter of the way into the novel, Melville devotes two entire chapters to Moby Dick—an attempt to grapple with the reality and meaning of this whale—"Moby Dick" and "The Whiteness of the Whale." Ishmael as narrator has been interested in exploring what Moby Dick means in retrospect, *Moby-Dick* being told as a reminiscence. All the material presented about whales and whaling, then, is an attempt to discover the meaning of Ahab's quest and Ishmael's own experience as a crew member of the *Pequod*. Ishmael sees naught in that whale but the deadliest ill. Unlike Ahab, Ishmael does not consider Moby Dick his enemy. Ahab, however, believes that the world is controlled either by a vicious God who operates through visible objects represented by Moby Dick, or is controlled possibly by nothing—that there is nothing behind the mask. We must remember how blasphemous these two beliefs were in Melville's pious century, which explains why Melville depended on irony and evasiveness so much. Actually, much of what is thought about Moby Dick is based on heresay, rumor, fears, and superstitions; legend has it that Moby Dick is ubiquitous and immortal. What is true for certain is that Moby Dick is powerful, larger than most sperm whales, with a snow-white forehead, a high white hump on his back, and a deformed, scythe-like lower jaw.

In the famous "Whiteness of the Whale" chapter, Ishmael tells us that for him, Moby Dick's whiteness was the most appalling characteristic and suggests that the whiteness provokes terror in humans because it cannot be explained or grasped. Whiteness is awful because "by its indefiniteness it shadows forth the heartless voids and immensities of the universe." Whiteness, therefore, suggests annihilation, meaninglessness, universal indifference. The fear whiteness provokes, then, is primal, beyond rationality. Ishmael warns us not to be too curious about this leviathan since it is one creature in the world which must remain unpainted to the last. Moby Dick's voracity is seen as natural; that is, the sea is full of universal cannibalism. Ishmael suggests that we are part of this universal cannibalism; therefore, Ahab wants to destroy a force that has been a natural part of the universe long before human beings existed, when the whale was king of the earth.

Whatever moral or metaphysical significance Moby Dick might have, it is its physicality, its sheer omnipresence, that must be recognized. Ishmael views Moby Dick with a sense of mystery. Here is a phenomenon of existence that defies rational explanation; thus, it is to be regarded with respect, an object of profound curiosity. The whale, in short, is terrifying, powerful, inscrutable.

What Ahab fails to realize is that much of the evil perpetrated is caused by human beings. There are indifferent evils like natural disasters and disease, but Ahab projects evil onto visible objects, thereby abdicating any personal sense of responsibility for evil in the universe. Ironically, it is Fleece, the aged Negro cook, bossed around by the mindless Stubb, who understands the connection between humanity and sharks (he calls the sharks "fellow-critters"). In the "Stubb's Supper" chapter, Fleece preaches to the sharks to govern their sharkishness, for "all angel is not'ing more dan de shark well goberned." "Your woraciousness, fellow-critters, I don't blame ye so much for; dat is natur, and can't be helped; but to gobern dat wicked natur, dat is de pint." The chapter ends with Fleece's sage ejaculation about Stubb: "more of shark dan Massa Shark hisself." The lines between master and slave and predator and prey certainly become blurred. While it is easier to project evil onto others, Melville insists we must recognize the shark within us and try to govern it, not eliminate it, since that is against nature. As Melville said in *Mardi:* "All evils cannot be done away. For evil is the chronic malady of the universe; and checked in one place, breaks forth in another." Here Melville is echoing Hawthorne's view about evil, a decidedly anti-Transcendental one, which is the theme of Hawthorne's famous short story "Young Goodman Brown": "The fiend in his own shape is less hideous than when he rages in the breast of man." Goodman Brown, like Ahab, Pip, Nathan, and Sophie, is destroyed by the knowledge of demonism in the world.

This brings us to the portrayal of evil in *Sophie's Choice,* an evil that remains frustratingly mysterious for all of us—the Holocaust—represented by Sophie's "all but incomprehensible history." Like Moby Dick, the Holocaust is not mere symbol but a terrifying physical reality. The big difference, however, is that Moby Dick is a natural phenomenon, and the crematoria were created by human beings. Both novels ponder the mystery of iniquity, insisting that evil will always remain mysterious. Auschwitz must remain the one place on earth most unyielding to meaning or definition. How the Holocaust occurred is well documented; why it occurred remains a mystery, but that does not mean we must stop trying to come to terms with our evil potential. When the Nazis were not killing people, they were turning them into animals. Perhaps the worst legacy is that those who managed to survive feel guilty for having done so. Sophie's "badness" "pursued her like a demon"; she has a "schizoid conscience." Stingo finally acknowledges at the end of his voyage that Auschwitz will remain inexplicable to him and to all of humanity; absolute evil is never extinguished from the world.

Styron said this about evil when asked why he chose Malraux's quotation about absolute evil to serve as one of the novel's epigraphs:

> But what mystifies me, and it's very hard to express, is that we are all of a species, you and I and all of our ancestors, we came from the same womb, the same source and we are in effect brothers. But all the horror and suffering, aside from natural disasters which there is no way to explain, are caused by man, by our own species, acting in evil ways towards himself. It's a very simple, but a very complex equation. Nature is indifferent. You could say much of the evil that we feel is a product of irrational nature, disease, let's say cancer. There's no way of explaining it. It happens, and it's evil. And an earthquake, you could say, is a kind of indifferent evil, or a flood. These things are part of the natural scene, but, basically, the unhappiness and the things we all consider to be evil derive from ourselves.
>
> We who are supposed to be brothers are the authors of the pain and oppression of the world. And it's a mystery, because one would think that, theoretically, a species such as we are with our capacity for love and goodness and friendship, which we all have, most of us, unless we're crazy, so often are mechanized and twisted through society, politics, through a thousand different ways, into causing evil and suffering. It's a mystery but I think that's what a writer has to deal with. And I have. (West 232)

Melville had to write *Moby-Dick* partially in code since his vision was so blasphemous in 1850 in America. He said he had written a wicked book and felt proud. His reading of Shakespeare, particularly the Shakespeare of *King Lear* and *Hamlet,* confirmed his sense of the dark forces, of selfishness and cruelty, in human beings; he came to acknowledge that there was something arbitrary and irrational in the very structure of things. Melville had the courage to look at life without illusions, to demonstrate the dangers of refusing to question, revealing in the process the nobility of defiance. Too many Americans had opted for an empty innocence, an ignorance of evil, which is actually immaturity or spiritual cowardice; Starbuck's pious view, his "right reason," is revealed as shallow.

Just five years after the publication of *Moby-Dick,* Melville published *Benito Cereno,* an even darker tale about the dangers of ignorance and innocence. Yankee Captain Amasa Delano was another American with a "singularly undistrustful good nature, not liable, except in extraordinary and repeated incentives, and hardly then, to indulge in personal alarms, any way involving the imputation of malign evil in man." Captain Delano thinks Don Benito should be ecstatic because his life has been spared in the course of a slave mutiny on board his ship. Delano says, "You are saved," but Benito replies, "The negro." As long as human beings have memory, they can never be happy or innocent; innocence is cowardice.

This is critical for an understanding of Sophie. Her life has been spared, but she has memories to haunt her eternally despite her attempts to block these memories through alcohol, music, and sex. The young Stingo, with his "delusionary dreams about a Southern love nest" shared with Sophie, is a kind of Captain Delano, a present-oriented American, divorced from history, from maturity. Stingo thinks he can erase her past by sweeping her away to his peanut farm in Virginia, marrying her, and having children with her. The thought of becoming a wife and mother again, however, causes Sophie to feel ill: she has too many horrific memories of losing her children to the crematoria and her husband to a Nazi firing squad. How can a woman like Sophie truly start over?

There are many survivors today who have seemingly started over, but their nightmare world continues to haunt them. Many survivors suffer extreme psychic disorders and, sadly, sometimes pass their pain on to their children. Many children of survivors have trouble reading *Sophie's Choice* objectively, accusing Styron of anti-Semitism and intruding immorally on their territory. Their parents' pain has thoroughly become their pain; they find it obscene to try to understand those who perpetrated this pain. In fact, a meeting of children of survivors in New York City recently condemned Styron for giving a Gentile, Sophie, the "luxury" of a choice. Clearly, the evil that is the Holocaust continues to cause suffering and madness. For many, the Holocaust is the central event of the twentieth century with which we must grapple. Stingo cannot weep for eleven million people, but he can weep for Sophie, Nathan, Jan, Eva, Eddie Farrell, Bobby Weed, Artiste, Maria Hunt, Nat Turner, and Wanda, "just a few of the beaten and butchered and betrayed and martyred children of the earth." Melville and Styron show us that war is indeed humanity's madness, a fall from our inborn creative potential.

Those who dive too deeply, those whose sense of evil is so inflexible and adamant in their refusal to admit any existent good, come perilously close to a love of evil, to a queer pact with the devil. Ahab's last words are: "Oh, lonely death on lonely life! Oh, now I feel my topmost greatness lies in my topmost grief." Ahab and Nathan, Promethean in their defiance, push the quest too far. Both *Moby-Dick* and *Sophie's Choice* demonstrate that our greatness must not lie in our topmost grief. After experiencing the most profound rage, sorrow, and despair, after fully understanding our lonely, abandoned place in the universe, we must still conquer grief and affirm the dignity of life. Both Ishmael and Stingo learn this by the end of their journeys.

Sophie, and many other Holocaust survivors, can never conquer their grief and fully rejoin the living. How can they forgive their tormentors, forgive the murder of millions? It is hard not to recall the recent suicide of Primo Levi, the Italian novelist, chemist, and Holocaust survivor, or the many Vietnam veterans who will never fully rejoin the living. One of the most bitter legacies of the Holocaust is that many survivors feel evil and guilt-ridden themselves. Sophie, therefore, does not have the choice that Ahab has.

A recent book called *Haing Ngor: A Cambodian Odyssey* by Dr. Haing Ngor, the Cambodian physician who won an Academy Award for his performance in the film *The Killing Fields,* grapples with the human capacity for evil. His book explores Cambodia's exercise in auto-genocide. The Khmer Rouge tried to exterminate or at least deliberately work to death a majority of the population systematically, a regime which makes even less sense than the Third Reich. Ngor admits he does not understand the Khmer Rouge, his own people. Confronting the Cambodian capacity for evil, we cannot but wonder about our own. For most of us, "the face of evil will remain as blank as the stare of a patrolling shark" (Nordland).

Another new book, a novel entitled *The Immortal Bartfuss* by Aharon Appelfeld, Israeli novelist and Holocaust survivor, paints a portrait of a man who survived the Holocaust and now resides in Israel. Appelfeld explores a survivor's mysterious and hallucinatory private being, reminiscent of Camus' *The Stranger,* but even more extreme in its vision of alienation. Bartfuss is called immortal because "there are fifty bullets in his body." We are to understand Bartfuss as being not so much alive as merely undead. He feels like a shadow and hates his wife for having given birth to children who force him to become more than a survivor, a stranger. Bartfuss thinks that he could have been happy were it not for his wife and children, if he could live on an island alone. However he discovers a need to love, to give, to reenter the human family through his daughter Bridget. Bartfuss offers to buy his daughter a watch, acknowledging the value of time, the fullness of human existence. He can still act, can still love. Appelfeld shows the need for survivors and, in effect, for all of us, to live as if—as if there is a way out of the nightmare. In an interview with Philip Roth, Appelfeld said his latest novel "offers its survivor [Bartfuss] neither Zionist nor religious consolation." Bartfuss has "no advantage over anyone else, but he still hasn't lost his human face. That isn't a great deal, but it's something" (Roth 31).

Melville and Styron offer neither Zionist nor religious consolation in their dark novels. *Moby-Dick* begins Christmas day, but evil remains despite the birth of a savior. Our lives are "encompassed by all the horrors of the half known life." Yet both *Moby-Dick* and *Sophie's Choice* have somewhat optimistic epilogues, both of which have been misinterpreted. Many critics have argued that the only reason Ishmael is rescued at the end is so that there can be a survivor to tell the tale. That misses, however, the important symbolism of the brief epilogue. Ishmael is literally buoyed up by Queequeg's coffin, so that the ship *Rachel,* searching after her missing children, "only found another orphan." Ishmael is still the lonely outcast he was at the beginning of the novel but with one major difference: he has experienced firsthand the meaning of love, death, evil, and madness. He undergoes a conversion to the subversive. Metaphorically, Ishmael is saved because he has fully accepted his humanity, adopting a doctrine of racial and social community as an ideal to set opposite the isolated individual; Ishmael's embrace of a black pagan represents a protest against civilized hypocrisy. Queequeg is loyal to his beliefs and friendships. He has risked his life to save his shipmate Tashtego and, of course, his symbolic loyalty at the end of the novel, his coffin, saves Ishmael's life. Through his friendship with Queequeg, Ishmael feels a melting. "No more my splintered heart and maddened hand were turned against this wolfish world." Ishmael comes to respect the "common continent of men." If we all walk into the jaws of the whale, lucky is any person who has a real friend. We are indeed enveloped in whale-lines, lines which link whalesmen to their prey and can destroy them as it does Ahab, but which also link Ishmael to Queequeg, to communal effort, to loyalty, to love; we have both options.

We must remember that Ishmael is reborn, but he is still an orphan. Ishmael's survival is absurd in a universe ruled by a capricious God or no God at all; alienation remains the central theme. What is important, though, is that Ishmael makes a pro-life choice while conscious of his dissatisfactions, yearnings, and homelessness, conscious that all of us are limited by necessity and chance; he has conquered his suicidal despair. Melville suggests that there is a certain kind of serenity in knowing one's limits and maintaining one's dignity, in accepting one's destiny as an orphan in the universe. Ishmael learns to accept the world without understanding all of it. Melville, then, saves Ishmael from pious Christianity and primitive Pantheism.

Ishmael's acceptance of his vulnerable humanity is reflected in the vision of nature in the epilogue: "The unharming sharks, they glided by as if with padlocks on their mouths; the savage seahawks sailed with sheathed beaks." The symbolic linking of Ishmael and Queequeg projects an ideal of interracial harmony, a power to counterbalance the sharks and seahawks, the way to "gobern" the shark within. It is a power that comes from a defiance of, not submission to, Christian orthodoxy. The resurrection at the end of *Moby-Dick,* then, is humanistic and accidental, not religious; the pulpit does not lead the world. That is the meaning of Ishmael's voyage of discovery. Only a humane, broadly tolerant view and defiance give meaning to a life that seems a meaningless, unfriendly ocean.

Similarly, the longer epilogue in *Sophie's Choice,* which Stingo calls "A Study in the Conquest of Grief," reveals the meaning of Stingo's voyage of discovery. Stingo is sickened by the hypocrisy and witlessness of the Reverend DeWitt, who delivers the eulogy for Sophie and Nathan, both of whom he did not know, pompously declaring Sophie and Nathan "lost children. Victims of an age of rampant materialism. Loss of universal values. Failure of the old-fashioned principles of self-reliance." What a bitter irony to blame their deaths on the failure of self-reliance. Did not Sophie and Nathan suffer because of self-reliance gone mad, individualism turned into totalitarian madness, the blind will to power? Religious consolation is nothing more than hypocrisy, immaturity, and mendacity.

Stingo, therefore, will not let the Reverend have the last word. He reads the poetry of Emily Dickinson, the poet who brought Sophie and Nathan together, appropriate as well because Dickinson's poetry reveals her own profound religious doubts. Stingo knows how much classical music meant to Sophie and Nathan and was, therefore, appalled that "no one had bothered to consult about the music, and this was both an irony and a shame." The grandeur of Brahms was replaced by the peevishness and vulgarity of Gounod's "Ave Maria." Stingo knows that it is art, not religion, that affirms our existence, our dignity.

Stingo tells us that his very survival was in question after the deaths of Sophie and Nathan. It is at this extreme point of suicidal despair that Stingo comes to understand that no one can understand Auschwitz, that absolute evil will never be extinguished. The sharks and seahawks will always be there. If there is any hope, any bearable truth, it is in loving all living things. "Let your love flow out on all living things." Is this possible after Auschwitz? Did not Auschwitz alter the nature of love entirely? Is not love absurd in a world "which permitted the black edifice of Auschwitz to be built"? Stingo admits it is too early to answer that question, but he remembers "some fragile yet perdurable hope."

Stingo wants to lose himself after the funeral and goes back to Coney Island. Wanting to drown, he begins to cry instead. He now has the wisdom that is woe, the painful memories, the rage and sorrow for all the butchered children. Stingo falls into a disturbed sleep and dreams of drowning in a whirling vortex of mud, buried alive, almost drowned in a vortex like Ishmael. When Stingo awakens, however, he discovers he has been covered with sand, not suffocating mud, by children trying to protect him. Stingo has been spared annihilation because of the instinctive compassion of children, who find randomly, like the *Rachel* did, another orphan. Stingo blesses his resurrection, understanding that this was "not judgment day— only morning. Morning: excellent and fair." For a while at least, the sharks have padlocks on their mouths, and the savage seahawks sail with sheathed beaks. Again, the resurrection is not religious but humanistic; *Moby-Dick* and *Sophie's Choice* are essentially anti-Christian novels. If there is to be any resurrection, it will come from an affirmation of human dignity despite an awareness of the wisdom that is woe, a wisdom that Ishmael and Stingo initially try to avoid but later come to embrace.

It is interesting to note here that Stingo is reading *Billy Budd* at the beginning of his journey. It is at the end of his journey that he will be fully able to understand that novella about paternal and fraternal love gone astray, about the dangers of submission and obedience. Billy is falsely accused by fellow shipmate Claggart and condemned to hang by Captain Vere, whose rigid formalism overshadows his paternal feelings for Billy, the foundling. Both Melville and Styron dramatize the horrors of malicious or illegal authority and the subsequent need for and dignity of revolt, be it a revolt against a cruel cosmos as in *Moby-Dick* or human tyranny as in *Billy Budd* and *Sophie's Choice.*

This brings us to Styron's link to Camus, the twentieth-century writer whose work is closely associated with the need to affirm human dignity in the face of a meaningless universe, and Camus' link to Melville. Camus, like Styron, was influenced by Melville's mighty themes; he was more comfortable in his unbelief, however, than Melville. All three novelists can be called obstinate humanists, affirmative and moral in the face of a Machiavellian universe. Camus' favorite American novelist was Melville, and the only twentieth-century American writer he admired was Faulkner. Twentieth-century American literature for him was guilty of crude realism, a *littérature de l'élémentaire.* Camus felt that nineteenth-century grandeur, as exemplified by the works of Melville, was replaced by magazine writing in which the interior life was simply ignored, in which human beings were described but never explained. Twentieth-century American literature was documentation, not art, which he attributed to the commercialization of literature.

Camus was profoundly influenced, however, by *Moby-Dick,* which he called a truly absurd work. He read the novel in 1941 in the Gallimard edition shortly before he wrote his novel *The Plague.* From Melville he learned how symbol could be raised to the universal quality of myth. To dramatize the problem of evil, Camus chose a plague which was, like the whale, a symbol of evil. Camus, too, was intrigued by the character of Ishmael, the lonely, sea-loving wanderer. He wrote essays about Melville, his literary brother in pain, psychologically identifying with him. The interesting historical connection is that *The Plague* was written during the German occupation of France, and *Moby-Dick* was written when the Union was being torn apart by the slavery crisis. It is not surprising that both novelists would emphasize the need for human solidarity in their work. When Camus visited New York, he was most moved by the Bowery and not the skyscrapers. He was disturbed by the American attitude toward the black race, another link to Melville, and saw to it that Richard Wright was translated and published in Paris. Having been born Algerian, Camus was particularly sensitive to illegal and malicious authority, to feeling victimized because of race. And having been a part of the Resistance movement in German-occupied France, Camus was fully acquainted with evil and death, acquainted in a way most Americans are not.

Aware of the horrors of existence, Camus preached revolt, but not Byronic or Marxist revolt: that way lies nihilism and police terror. A person who refuses to lie, for Camus, is a person in revolt. Rebellion, then, implies tension, incompletion, and no absolutes. Most rebels, he claimed, choose the comfort of tyranny or servitude. While intelligence must always be in revolt against a hostile universe, tyranny which authorizes murder is unacceptable, and nihilism, which values nothing and flirts with the apocalypse, leads to suicide. Camus had contempt for the cowardice of submission. The answer to murder and suicide is a rebellion against suffering to promote healing. Human love must be thought an end in itself.

Camus criticized American authors who created characters with no memories and no understanding of the past and future, characters defined only by immediate sensations. Melville and Camus, however, were able to dramatize the tragedy of human existence while also providing limited but honest affirmations. Underneath a Melville or Camus is a rigorous idealism, but one which has been painfully extracted, not the "unearned unhappiness" Sophie bitterly rebukes in the Americans she meets in 1947.

It was unusual for a nineteenth-century American writer, for Melville, to understand that Americans cannot transcend or escape history, to rebuke America for its resistance to the painful process of growing up. Many American writers of the nineteenth century preferred their heroes to be liberated from family and social history, morally prior to the world, American Adams. *Moby-Dick* is actually a total blasting of the vision of innocence of the moral childishness of the hopeful. In Melville's works we see Adam gone mad with disillusion. This is all the more remarkable since the era of the 1840s was a time when hopefulness was all the fashion, like this century's 1940s. Melville deeply felt the agony of living in an America where empty-headed cheerfulness was a religion, and so he leaned on European tradition, on a tragic conception which understood that creativity itself is associated with a monstrous vision of evil, that artists get their strength from an acknowledgment of evil.

Similarly, *Sophie's Choice* is a total blasting of the vision of innocence which demonstrates the impossibility of escaping or transcending history. The novel is set shortly after World War II, a time of great hopefulness and prosperity. Americans were heroes, with America having emerged as the major superpower. At the beginning of the novel, Stingo has just returned from his stint in Okinawa. To many Americans, the Second World War was a war against the Japanese. What Stingo learns in that hopeful era of the 1940s is that while he was gorging on bananas in April of 1943, in an attempt to meet the minimum weight requirement for the U.S. Marines, Sophie and her two children were being carted to Auschwitz. America had been spared occupation, bombing, and invasion, but to be a European was to have experienced all three. Stingo must confront his, and, by extension, America's painful ignorance and childishness.

Stingo learns he is ignorant on many counts. He thought he would never hear another shot fired after World War II. He had never heard of Höss before he met Sophie. He thought Nathan's outbursts were a "shocking failure of character, a lapse of decency, rather than the product of some aberration of mind." Drug addicts were ax murderers to Stingo. He did not know enough to connect Nathan's dilated pupils with drug addiction, and madness to Stingo was "an unspeakable condition possessed by poor devils raving in remote padded cells." His ignorance and innocence was America's in the 1940s: "What Americans had been spared in our era.... How scant our count of fathers and sons compared to the terrible martyrdom of those unnumbered Europeans. Our glut of good fortune was enough to make us choke." Recently, the broadcaster Eric Sevareid said that news on television "has become part of the daily entertainment of a rather bored society.... If you had another great war or great depression, that would change matters, but that would be too high a price" ("Sevareid Assails TV News").

A tragic awareness must be forced if a civilization is to survive. In this, Styron most closely resembles Camus: both are twentieth-century writers who have accepted both the death of God and the meaninglessness and indifference of the universe while simultaneously affirming the values which the Nazis denied their victims. There may be no salvation, no eternal justice, but revolt can establish justice. While evil is mysterious, we must still resist its pull; the role of the artist is to look into the abyss, forcing a level of consciousness which has the potential for constructive action, not a nihilistic vision which denies action, denies the will. Camus and Styron paradoxically urge rebellion and moderation, eternal struggle, yet limits and incompletion. They are writers closer to the Greeks who knew that human beings are limited, closer to a Promethean vision of mankind's deliverance.

A speech Camus delivered in 1946 to students at Columbia University might very well serve as the philosophy that lies at the heart of *Sophie's Choice,* a viewpoint only a European living in occupied territory during World War II and active in the Resistance movement could have. It is this viewpoint that Stingo comes to share, prompted first by his association with Sophie and Nathan and later by experiencing the 1950s, 1960s, and 1970s—"wretched unending years of madness, illusion, error, dream, and strife." Camus said:

We were born at the beginning of the First World War. As adolescents we had the crisis of 1929; at twenty, Hitler. Then came the Ethiopian War, the Civil War in Spain, and Munich. These were the foundations of our education. Next came the Second World War, the defeat, and Hitler in our homes and cities. Born and bred in such a world, what did we believe in? Nothing. Nothing except the obstinate negation in which we were forced to close ourselves from the very beginning. The world in which we were called to exist was an absurd world, and there was no other in which we could take refuge. The world of culture was beautiful, but it was not real. And when we found ourselves face to face with Hitler's terror, in what values could we take comfort, what values could we oppose to negation? In none. If the problem had been the bankruptcy of a political ideology, or a system of government, it would have been simple enough. But what had happened came from the very root of man and society. There was no doubt about this, and it was confirmed day after day not so much by the behavior of the criminals but by that of the average man. The facts show that men deserved what was happening to them. Their way of life had so little value; and the violence of the Hitlerian negation was in itself logical. But it was unbearable and we fought it.

Now that Hitler has gone, we know a certain number of things. The first is that the poison which impregnated Hitlerism has not been eliminated; it is present in each of us. Whoever today speaks of human existence in terms of power, efficiency, and "historical tasks" spreads it. He is an actual or potential assassin. For if the problem of man is reduced to any kind of "historical task," he is nothing but the raw material of history, and one can do anything one pleases with him. Another thing we have learned is that we cannot accept any optimistic conception of existence, any happy ending whatsoever. But if we believe that optimism is silly, we also know that pessimism about the action of man among his fellows is cowardly.

We oppose terror because it forces us to choose between murdering and being murdered; and it makes communication impossible. This is why we reject any ideology that claims control over all of human life. (Chiaromonte 14–15)

It is curious that Camus was more admired here than in France for a time, having been criticized, especially by Sartre, for his anticommunist stand. Also, he rebuked France for its imperialism in his native Algeria, warning as early as 1939 what would happen if Algerian suffering continued to be ignored. Styron, who has been critical of the United States, has been criticized in America but has been terribly popular in France. Obviously, writers express thoughts their own readers hide from themselves. This certainly explains the popularity in France of Poe, Melville, and Faulkner as well. The best writers try to give body and voice to the tragic elements that society officially wishes to ignore.

Styron's career, in fact, resembles Camus' more than it does other American novelists. Styron is not only a novelist but a committed essayist, confronting the important political, social, and moral issues of his day. A collection of his moving nonfiction prose entitled *This Quiet Dust* was published in 1982 and closely resembles Camus' *Resistance, Rebellion, and Death*. Revealing Styron's engagement and commitment to public life, *This*

Quiet Dust addresses such issues as the death penalty, slavery, pornography, and the Holocaust. His fiction and nonfiction, like that of Camus, demonstrate a sense of moral responsibility, a knowledge of the sinister forces in history and modern life which threaten all of us. Not typically American, Styron does wed politics and literature, public and private concerns. Like Camus' essays, *This Quiet Dust* could serve as an entryway to Styron's fiction. Ironically, however, *This Quiet Dust* was diminished by some critics. One reviewer asserted that Styron's powers are largely rhetorical, that his eloquence and passion do the work of thought. Melvin J. Friedman, contributor of many pieces on Styron and a book-length study of his fiction, however, said this about Styron's fate as an artist:

> This least parochial of contemporary American writers appears fated to have each of his books underestimated and misunderstood at home and then warmly accepted abroad, especially in France. *This Quiet Dust* will surely one day have a place next to Mann's *Essays of Three Decades*, Valéry's *History and Politics*, and Camus's *Resistance, Rebellion, and Death*—where it belongs. (37)

What is important here is that *Sophie's Choice* owes more to European philosophy than to American thinking, a fact which enables Styron to dramatize and criticize the American myth of Adamic innocence. It should be obvious that calling *Sophie's Choice* "Southern Gothic fiction" or "Holocaust Gothic" is painfully off the mark. Styron certainly does not "avoid the contraries" in his fiction. At the heart of the stark visions of Styron and Camus is "an invincible sun," not the Hollywood kind, but the kind that asserts that the universe is full of evil, and whatever good exists, exists in people. Still, life is a trial, and suffering and death are certain. Revolt alone can establish justice: revolt against the servitude of hope.

Here Camus and Styron are most at odds with Emerson, particularly Emerson's concept of compensation. Essentially, Emerson asserted that nobody can harm one but oneself, that nothing can be given or taken without an equivalent. It would be instructive to quote his short poem "Compensation" in its entirety:

> Why should I keep holiday
> When other men have none?
> Why but because, when these are gay,
> I sit and mourn alone?
>
> And why, when mirth unseals all tongues,
> Should mine alone be dumb?
> Ah! late I spoke to silent throngs,
> And now their hour is come. (Whicher 412)

Emerson also believed one's fortune, one's fate, to be the fruit of one's character. "The event is the print of your form," he wrote. As such, an individual's fortunes can never be inappropriate, cruel, or undeserved; we are all equally compensated. There is no room, then, for innocent suffering. *Sophie's Choice* stands as a rebuke to such a Transcendental view, revealing the horrific inequities of fate and the overwhelming suffering it causes. Sophie's fate is certainly not just the fruit of her character, nor was the fate of the millions of Jews and non-Jews gassed in the crematoria under Hitler's reign. The speaker in "Compensation" asks why he should be happy if others are not. The response is that when others are happy, he will "sit and mourn alone." Stingo, however, realizes the absurdity and horror of his having gorged on bananas while others were being gassed in Auschwitz; the simultaneity of events staggers his imagination. Should Stingo rest easy because some day he might know some unhappiness to compensate for the millions gassed? There can be no Emersonian compensation. Melville knew that the black race did not deserve its fate in nineteenth-century America, and Styron knows, as does the older Stingo, that millions of innocent people were victimized by totalitarian madness, that the twentieth century has been a particularly barbaric one of overwhelmingly undeserved suffering.

It is not enough just to rebuke Transcendental thought, to abhor the American tendency towards mindless optimism. Styron, like Camus, offers an alternative. In "The Myth of Sisyphus," Camus addresses the most basic question: if life has no meaning, if nature is indifferent and God is dead, why live? Addressing the question of suicide, "The Myth of Sisyphus" ultimately asserts that the only way we can transcend our absurd existence is by protesting against it. Revolt, then, is the key to Camus' thinking, to his notion of happiness, the meaning of life, and artistic creation. Since there is no religious salvation, no afterlife, Camus urges us to love this life, to love struggle, to live a life in which happiness is based on sacrifice and personal responsibility. Stingo tells us he is an agnostic brave enough "to resist calling on any such questionable gaseous vertebrate as the Deity even in times of travail and suffering." We could say that Camus and Styron are pessimists about humanity's destiny but optimists where the individual is concerned.

Camus said that contemporary belief is not based on science as it was in the late nineteenth century, but rather that it denies both science and religion. It is not the skepticism of reason in the presence of a miracle but passionate unbelief. We must, Camus insists, think of Sisyphus as being happy as he struggles once more to push that rock up the hill. The temptation of nihilism will always be present. The attempt to fight nihilism, however, can be seen in all of Styron's fiction, and it reaches a most poignant intensity in *Sophie's Choice,* given the Holocaust as its subject matter. Styron urges us to resist the temptation of absolutes as answers to the pain of existence. The Resistance worker in *Sophie's Choice,* Wanda, says that whether the Resistance saved Jews or not, they tried, and that is satisfaction. Likewise, the defiance behind Ahab's spear-hurling gesture is more significant than the gesture's futility.

Camus was acutely aware of our potential lethal will to power. Melville intuited this danger, and *Sophie's Choice* dramatizes the consequences of those who rationalize or justify absolute power. The new revolt must be a rebellion against the will to power. Evil, for Camus and Styron, stems from diffused guilt and the fatal mistake of the will to power. We must accept our orphaned state with its inevitable suffering and defeat and occasional triumphs. Hiding from this reality will result in either self-destructive or aggressive behavior, a need to dominate others. Melville says in *White-Jacket* that murder and suicide are the last resources of an insulted and unendurable existence. The resistance shown to the works of Melville and Styron in the United States reveals how uncharacteristically American is this view.

Styron has said that all of his fiction concentrates on victims of one sort or another and on the possibility for beauty in this absurd existence. *Sophie's Choice* confronts the victims of the Holocaust and offers the possibility of beauty and love after Auschwitz, a heroic stand. Most despair, including current cynicism, is fed on ugliness and violence. Camus and Styron insist that we must not exile beauty and love. Camus said, "There is beauty and there are the humiliated. Whatever may be the difficulties of the undertaking, I should like never to be unfaithful either to one or to the other" (*The Myth of Sisyphus and Other Essays* 145). If we compare this to what Styron says about the role of the novel we can see just how closely allied he is with Camus:

> In this fantastic world the claims on our emotions and our intellect are so urgent, so persistent and clamorous, that it is no longer either sufficient or rewarding to curl up with yet another cleverly written, well-crafted novel which describes, say, the beginning and the end of a love affair. During the novel's serene heyday the changes and varieties on this theme—and a score of other themes—might readily engross the reader's attention, but in our day they no longer suffice; we've been there too many times before. (West 156)

> Sartre was wrong. For me, if literature cannot change the world in a radical way, it can, all the same, penetrate deeply into human consciousness. Millions of people can read, and I believe that a book can work on their consciences. As a writer I have no other goal. (West 255)

Writers must continue their search for significant themes, but characters must not be allowed to succumb to theme. Melville, Camus, and Styron have sometimes allowed characters to succumb to theme, but *Sophie's Choice* is Styron's most satisfying novel in the sense that character, theme, and action are ideally blended to produce a great work of art which readers can regard with awe and have something in their lives that did not exist before. *Sophie's Choice* is that rarest of fictions: a novel which explores our national character that is not journalistic, ideological, or parochial.

Styron and Camus know that a period "which, in a space of fifty years, uproots, enslaves, or kills seventy million human beings should be condemned out of hand" (Camus, *The Rebel* 3); however, they both argue that this period and its culpability must be understood, that a belief in nothing justifies everything. As Camus says, "we would be free to stoke the crematory fires or to devote ourselves to the care of lepers" (*The Rebel* 5). Evil and virtue must never be considered mere chance or caprice. *Sophie's Choice* is an act of metaphysical rebellion protesting the human condition "both for its incompleteness, thanks to death, and its wastefulness, thanks to evil" (Camus, *The Rebel* 24). Camus feels the real passion of the twentieth century is servitude, a negation of everything, a rush towards an impossible innocence. In this sense, Camus can condemn Hitler's Germany and Stalin's Soviet Union, any utopian messianism, and, of course, America's own brand of innocence which, rather than seeing history as supreme, ignores its importance altogether. Rebellion is the refusal to be treated like an object, the refusal to be reduced to simple historical terms. When we put limits on history, we are giving birth to values. Camus states that "instead of killing and dying in order to produce the being that we are not, we have to live and let live in order to create what we are" (*The Rebel* 252). The novel, then, must be the literature of rebellion, not the literature of consent.

We can see the quest for unity, for affirming interior reality, in the novels of Melville, Camus, and Styron. If "art is an impossible demand given expression and form, there is no genius in negation and pure despair" (Camus, *The Rebel* 271). Art teaches us that human beings cannot be explained solely by history, and *Sophie's Choice* is proof that we will never understand Auschwitz just by reading historical accounts of this tragedy, that horror can be apprehended only obliquely, through artistic distance. Artistic rebellion will always exist because falsehood, injustice, and violence will always exist. Stingo is finally able to conclude at the end of his journey that absolute evil is never extinguished from the world. The older Stingo knows that we continue to pay for slavery, for the sale of human beings, that the black edifice of Auschwitz will always haunt mankind. Since there will always be suffering, there will be outrage at that suffering; art and rebellion will die only with the last human being.

Sophie's Choice demonstrates artistically that none of the evils that totalitarianism claims to remedy is worse than totalitarianism itself. Totalitarianism is based on faith in a perfect future (a rush towards innocence) and murder. Melville, Camus, and Styron are artists who have eased the various forms of bondage weighing upon us, overcoming the temptation of hatred. Ishmael and Stingo, maddened by their anti-Christian perceptions, must overcome their potential for suicide. In 1957, Camus said the wager of his generation was to accept everything: "If we are to fail, it is better, in any case, to have stood on the side of those who choose life than on the side of those who are destroying" (*Resistance, Rebellion, and Death* 246). The loftiest work will always be that which maintains an equilibrium between reality and the artist's rejection of that reality. If, as Camus asserts, an artist's only justification is to speak up for those who cannot do so, Styron is amply justified with his *Sophie's Choice,* a novel which speaks up for "but a few of the beaten and butchered and betrayed and martyred children of the earth." The emancipatory force of art, then, threatens tyrants of the Left and the Right.

Melville, Camus, and Styron have written mighty works because they have been drawn to mighty themes, particularly the themes of absurdity, evil, slavery, revolt, and love. All three have looked into the abyss and forced their narrators to come up cold against the inferno while maintaining an affirmative vision of the "common continent of men." All three novelists assert that although we cannot comprehend the mysteries of existence and iniquity, we can resist iniquity's tug.

It would be instructive here to discuss briefly Conrad's disturbing turn-of-the-century novella, *Heart of Darkness,* which has interesting parallels with *Moby-Dick* and *Sophie's Choice.* Conrad was an early favorite of Styron, who at thirteen wrote an imitation Conrad short story entitled "Typhoon and the Tor Bay," and whose unfinished novel, *The Way of the Warrior,* abandoned when Styron felt compelled to write *Sophie's Choice* instead, has been compared to *Lord Jim.* Conrad, Styron told this writer, has saturated his thought and has been a helpful influence on his work. Whereas *Moby-Dick* is a revolt against a cruel cosmos, *Heart of Darkness* and *Sophie's Choice* are more concerned with the varieties of human evil, acknowledging the "heart of an immense darkness." *Moby-Dick, Heart of Darkness,* and *Sophie's Choice* are symbolic journeys into our darker regions, written as reminiscences so the cool light of intelligence can play over them.

Besides similarities in theme and narrative strategies, there are fascinating connections among the characters in these three works. Kurtz, a man relieved of all social and civilized restraints, touches bottom after committing himself to the total pursuit of evil and depravity. He is a Promethean protagonist, grandly demonic, a man whose grandiose, idealistic mission degenerates into barbarism and domination. Ahab and Nathan are also grandly demonic figures whose observations tear them apart. Marlow is in the middle; he is shaken by peering into the abyss but does not go mad like Kurtz. He is also philosophical like Ahab, but he does not let his observations tear him apart, although he comes perilously close to the edge by his own admission, drawing back his foot from the precipice of madness. Marlow's confrontation with an individual's capacity for evil leaves him sober, disturbed, meditative, and obsessed with relating his story. Similarly, Stingo and Ishmael, the lone survivors of their tales, are left shaken after their confrontation with demonism but come to accept our potential for evil and good. Ishmael, Marlow, and Stingo, while irrevocably changed because of their journeys, leaving them little to cheer about, emerge nevertheless affirming human dignity. Though these narrators escape, they learn wisdom at a price—the wisdom that is woe. Their rejection of fantacism, their wisdom, makes these narrators seem pale and anonymous in comparison with the charismatic figures of Ahab, Kurtz, and Nathan. *Moby-Dick, Heart of Darkness,* and *Sophie's Choice,* then, explore our capacity for evil as well as our ability to resist it, the necessity for restraint (to "gobern de shark"), and the need to conquer grief.

   Despite the tragic nature of our existence, Melville, Camus, and Styron doggedly assert the dignity of humanity against the inexorable flux of history. If life copies art, it is possible these humanistic values will be emulated—the only antidote to the murders and suicides that flood the fictions of these novelists and our daily newspapers. The only way for us to become more human is for artists to create audacious works of fiction which make the human face richer and more admirable, lest we all drown in the vortex of atomic fallout.

   We must remember that *Sophie's Choice* was written from 1974 to 1979, a time of moral bankruptcy—the post-Vietnam, post-Watergate era. It is, therefore, a weary voice we hear in the older Stingo who tells a story about the 1940s but reflects the madness of the whole post-Holocaust era as well. If we read Styron's collection of essays, *This Quiet Dust,* we can glimpse Styron's concerns in the 1970s when he was writing *Sophie's Choice.* The Vietnam War's degeneracy was represented, for Styron, by Lieutenant Calley, whom he compares to Eichmann—two banal, witless nobodies claiming to be cogs in great machines. Styron writes that Calley had a choice, especially since other officers refused to follow Captain Ernest Medina's orders to kill everything in My Lai. Calley had no remorse. Evil is shown as a kind of diffused guilt, but even in war there must be codes, especially since for many men war is still the ultimate adventure, a means of escaping an ordinary existence. *Sophie's Choice* dramatizes the poet Marianne Moore's feelings, "There never was a war that wasn't inward." War is the madness in humanity. Styron has dedicated himself to writing about this catastrophic propensity of human beings to dominate and destroy each other, becoming an analyst of evil, claiming that Auschwitz is embedded in our cultural traditions, a sleeping virus which did not end with the destruction of the crematoria in 1945. We can never rest easy because totalitarianism is a constant threat to the human family. To attempt to come to terms with Auschwitz, we must consider Jew and non-Jew, victim and victimizer. Shortly before the publication of *Sophie's Choice*, Styron said: "We shall perhaps never even begin to understand the Holocaust until we are able to discern the shadows of the enormity looming beyond the enormity we already know" (*This Quiet Dust* 105).

Styron says that he is amazed that he is as political as he is since he began as a writer who was ivory-tower oriented. Over the years, he says, "I have almost unconsciously let my work be connected with politics, with politics insofar as they govern history and human affairs" (Caputo 140). It was being recalled into active duty during the Korean War that wrenched him out of his rarefied world, that taught him how the authoritarian mind works. Styron dissects not only military authority but any form of human domination. Styron claims that his fiction does not have a strong sense of place (except for *Lie Down in Darkness*), that this lack of a milieu forced him to cast around for themes. As demonstrated, he, like Melville, goes after big fish. He attributes his attraction to big themes to his conviction that history is a "marvelous and clear mirror of human behavior" (Caputo 150). His work harks back to the nineteenth century, when story and character were preeminent. It is no wonder, then, that he criticizes postmodernists who are obsessed with language and technique almost to the exclusion of story and character, traditionally considered the heart and soul of literature. Styron contends that "great literature, great in the sense that it endures, is the art of creating characters whom people do not want to consign to oblivion" (Caputo 154).

There have been eminent American literary critics who have asserted that America and its fictional characters have escaped history, critics like R. W. B. Lewis in *The American Adam*, Richard Chase in *The American Novel and Its Traditions*, and Richard Poirier in *A World Elsewhere*. Actually, however, our literary texts do present a response to history and social reality. In the mid-nineteenth century, American authors had to come to terms with a rising capitalist society and its resulting alienation. Melville and Styron, in particular, dramatize that alienation is the dominant social condition in modern history. Some American authors and fictional characters, however, have not been able to reconcile themselves to being alienated. Certainly we see this in Melville, Faulkner, and Styron, writers who insist that the novel be a powerful ideological form positioning itself against alienation, loneliness, and industrialization, against all the dehumanizing symptoms of modern life. These writers know that novelists are speakers, not just alienated spectators, that a writer cannot hide behind subjectivist idealism or objectivist materialism.

Sophie's story, therefore, reveals the inadequacies of Emerson's projection of self-reliance, exposing the consequences of Emerson's denial of the flesh, the family, and the social relatedness of every individual in the human community. The rope which binds all of us permits no mastership, only mutual dependence. Ahab and Nathan, although grand and sympathetic defiers, ultimately, because of their deep wounds, deny the human family, and, of course, the Holocaust represents the total breakdown of any notion of the human family. It is important, then, that Ishmael and Stingo are not merely spectators but observing participants in the action, albeit Stingo much more so than Ishmael, whose role is more that of an ironic expositor. Modern novelists and their fictional alter egos must be active participants, not merely alienated spectators who refuse to see their own implications in social history. Melville, Camus, and Styron, then, share an important similarity in the way they view the role of the artist in modern society: they take their characters seriously, endowing them with tragic freedom, allowing them to work on their fates under narrow limits, forcing them to confront the full tragic condition of life. There may be no religious redemption, but fiction can compensate humanity for the inadequacy of the religious vision.

How much more alienated can an individual be than Styron's portrait of the Commandant of Auschwitz, Rudolph Höss, who is unable to feel remorse or have any sympathy for his victims? Evil is shown as the inability to feel guilt for one's actions. Any Nazis who were a bit squeamish drank to ease their discomfort or blamed the Jews for making them feel uncomfortable. In contrast, Styron provides us with a portrait of Jozef, the young Resistance worker, who vomited and nearly went insane when he had to kill an informer. This also helps to explain Styron's characterization of Dr. Jemand von Niemand, the doctor from nowhere, who, by forcing Sophie to choose which child would live and which would die, wants to experience guilt to become human again. Since the Nazis had no identification with their victims, they focused not on what horrible things they did to people but on what horrible things they had to watch in pursuance of their duties.

Sophie's Choice suggests that unless we can put ourselves in the victim's shoes, we are doomed to commit evil acts. Stingo's father understands this very well. He makes the young Stingo stay in a freezing shed to show him what it was like for his mother to be left with inadequate coal heating; Stingo's punishment fits the crime exactly. One of Styron's unique contributions in *Sophie's Choice*, then, is the double vision of the victim and victimizer. *Sophie's Choice* forces us to confront the fact that victims can also become victimizers. Nathan is part Jewish victim, part Rudolph Höss. The fact that Sophie can have moments of virulent anti-Semitism is an index of the degree of horror which the camps and crematoria represent. This victim/victimizer syndrome is thus not limited to the sane or insane, not in a world that has seen the Final Solution. Stingo comes to understand this duality, this tragic compulsion, through Sophie and Nathan, and his understanding enables him to write his first novel, *Inheritance of Night,* about the South's duality. Styron, as critic Frederick Stern says,

> lets the horror be seen not from the center of the charnel house but from those who can share the motivations of the perpetrators of evil, even though they are also its victims. . . . Styron's choice is to try to understand the Holocaust, its perpetrators, and its awesome dead millions, by pointing out that victims can be victimizers and victimizers victims, in a complex interaction which is human and which we must understand if we are to have any hope of avoiding another such horror. What writer can be better equipped to undertake this task than a southerner who has left the South behind? (26–27)

Stingo is able to identify with the victim; an American can feel European, can feel his own hollowness. When sweeping Sophie away from the crazed Nathan to a supposed southern love nest, Stingo says this about Washington, D. C.: "Washington suddenly appeared paradigmatically American, sterile, geometrical, unreal. I had identified so completely with Sophie that I felt Polish, with Europe's putrid blood rushing through my arteries and veins. Auschwitz still stalked my soul as well as hers. Was there no end to this? No end?" To complement this feeling, Stingo notices the "hollow, Protestant ring" of church bells outside their Washington hotel.

The consequences of not being able to identify with victims are dramatized in profound ways in the novel, the most obvious of which is the Holocaust itself. There are also subtler evils evidenced by this lack of identification, scapegoating in general being one of them. Styron demonstrates how easy it is to blame others for one's misfortunes. While Hitler certainly did this on a large scale, Stingo and Sophie do this on a smaller scale. When Stingo's apartment is robbed, leaving him virtually penniless, he puts the blame on Morris Fink, a Jewish scapegoat for Stingo's misfortune. It is important, therefore, that it is Jewish Nathan who impulsively and generously gives Nathan two-hundred dollars to be repaid only if Stingo becomes a famous author. In weak moments, particularly after a violent fight with Nathan, Sophie blames the Jews for all her troubles. On a larger scale, Stingo concludes that Poland and the American South are similar in that their pride and their recollections of past glories are bulwarks against the humiliation of defeat. Poland blamed the Jews, and the South blamed the blacks for their troubles.

Related to the scapegoating tendency is stereotyping people or places to avoid thought. Nathan assumes Stingo is a cracker because he is from the South. Later, Nathan realizes: "How can I really have hated a place I have never seen or known?" An identification with the entire human community would prevent stereotyping and scapegoating, would have prevented the black edifice of Auschwitz.

Styron insists that it is we who are cruel, not Fortune. We commit evil when we try to control Fortune. This "fortune-forcing" is what critic John Kenny Crane focuses on in his book entitled *The Root of All Evil: The Thematic Unity of William Styron's Fiction,* published in 1984. Crane contends that the solitary pursuit of Fortune has repressed our natural instincts of empathy and identification. The remedy is the ability to turn away from the "lonely quest of Fortune's rewards" towards a fellowship with our fellow human beings, against the atrocities Fortune offers. It is not enough to know simply that evil and misery are going on while we are happy; we must experience the evil in order to squeeze evil into our hearts and souls— clearly the opposite of Emersonian compensation. The older Stingo is aware of this: "What had old Stingo been up to while Jozef and Sophie and Wanda had been writhing in Warsaw's unspeakable Gehenna? Listening to Glenn Miller, swilling beer, horsing around in bars, whacking off! God, what an iniquitous world."

Styron insists on Manichean dualism, demonstrating that human evil begins with the misuse of the less fortunate by Fortune's darlings. The young Stingo is one of Fortune's darlings, a potential misuser of the less fortunate; by extension, America is seen as Fortune's darling, a potential abuser. What saves Stingo from being an abuser, besides his ability to empathize with the sorrows of others, is having a father whose strong, coherent, moral sense provides a model Stingo can emulate. Stingo's father urges Stingo to cling to a stable moral center, to retain his humanity. But most of the fathers in Styron's fiction play God, and, attempting to force Fortune, are locked into self-destructive behavior. Stingo knows he is fortunate to have a father whom he can respect if not always agree with. Stingo's father demonstrates that it is possible to maintain a decent, loving sympathy in a selfish age. Nathan's brother, Larry, is another decent, loving individual, as are the young Resistance fighters, Wanda and Jozef. That they are all minor characters is the bitter point.

While some evils are curable, we are not meant to think that Stingo's vision of potential human goodness at the end of *Sophie's Choice* is absolute. The post-Holocaust years, the 1940s through the 1970s, according to the older Stingo, were "wretched unending years of madness, illusion, error, dreams, and strife." Stingo, however, looks forward with information that

Nathan and Sophie lacked when they made their critical mistakes and choices. Stingo, the lone survivor, may be less grand than Nathan, but like Ishmael he is courageous in his pro-life choice, given what he has learned during his voyage of discovery.

The good person, then, is the one who finds goodness within and develops it towards others. Ahab, Sophie's father, and Rudolph Höss cannot do this, with obvious catastrophic results. Wanda and Jozef, however, the two young Resistance fighters, are able to find this goodness, this ability to identify with those suffering. Sophie thinks that while the Nazis are rounding up Jews she and her children will be safe. Wanda knows that no one is safe or free when human beings tyrannize the less fortunate, which meant in Europe in the 1940s not only Jews but Poles, Slavs, Gypsies, homosexuals, and the mentally and physically handicapped—all enemies of the Third Reich. Wanda, a non-Jew, forces Sophie to look at pictures of the bodies of all the innocent children gassed, to see that the concentration camps were not just labor camps but extermination camps. The final irony is that the daughter and two grandchildren of one of the masterminds of the Final Solution, Sophie's father, experience firsthand the charnel house designed for Jews. Her father, Bieganski, "failed to foresee how such sublime hatred could only gather into its destroying core, like metal splinters sucked toward some almighty magnet, countless thousands of victims who did not wear the yellow badge." When we contrast Stingo's father with Sophie's we can see that the "progenitors of each new generation" must be held accountable for "the continued evolution of human evil" (Crane 118). Most young people who populate Styron's fictions have no decent parental figure to suggest a better direction than crass materialism, ugliness, and immorality. Sophie knows instinctively that all of her problems began with her father. What did the fathers of the SS officers teach them? Many officers admitted to being battered children. It is not surprising, then, that some would become butchers.

Why *Sophie's Choice* is so artistically successful, for Crane, is that it is Styron's most full-fledged plot in the narrative present with a more developed transcendent present since the narrator has researched his topic and shares his opinions on the findings and meaning of his 1947 experiences. The major flashbacks are actually a search for instructive memories. Because the novel is told as a reminiscence, the narrator must be able to shift time frames easily. Crane contends that Styron was able to make the narrative present as dramatic as the major flashbacks, so the past is given an active meaning in the present, enabling the narrator and the reader to redirect it. This narrative strategy reveals an ability to view the world from many perspectives, a view that is liberating. Consequently, Styron merges theme and action into a satisfying, unified whole.

Styron urges that we see ourselves as part of a life force—a force which compels us toward good, toward the preservation of the species, toward the "birthright ... to try to free people into the condition of love" (*Set This House on Fire* 362). Self-destruction, the wish for death, is the primary moral sin. The single good is the respect for the force of life. If evil is anything which is antilife, then, Styron makes it clear that the Holocaust was not just anti-Semitic but antilife; therefore, German and other historical revisionists who claim that the Holocaust never existed are evil because they, too, are antilife. That the Holocaust occurred at all is horrific beyond literal description; that some historians and others continue to try to rewrite history to obliterate the existence of the Holocaust is fortune-forcing of such frightening proportions that we are all at risk.

Both Melville and Styron demonstrate the dangers of mythmaking, the dangers of not being able to see things as they really are. For different reasons, Nathan and Sophie lie, rewriting their painful pasts. We are reminded, too, of *Billy Budd,* the novella which Stingo was reading at the beginning of his journey, particularly the penultimate chapter which provides a British newspaper account of what happened on board the *Bellipotent,* a clear attempt to rewrite history; the newspaper report contends that Billy was not an Englishman but some alien adopting an English cognomen who stabbed Claggart, the master-at-arms, to the heart. The evil revealed in this revisionist account is chilling.

Sophie's Choice is a novel which expresses outrage at the violence of authority and the submission of those who subscribe to it, as well as the pressure that its victims exert on the next generation to repeat the same mistakes. To revolt, as Camus said, is to refuse to lie, to refuse to be passive about suffering and evil; to revolt is to be fully engaged in history, in social reality. It is the liars who try to transcend, escape, or rewrite history.

We should be grateful, then, to our truthseekers—those artists who dive down into the blackest gorges and, like Melville's Catskill eagle, rise renewed from the ashes to soar higher than those who do not dive deeply. Styron agrees with Hardy that if a "way to the Better there be, it exacts a full look at the worst." This is what the early naturalistic novelists of the late nineteenth and early twentieth centuries did—delve deeply into the sordid in the hopes of finding remedies. Naturalism, then, had an idealistic, reformist strain which is all but dead today; Styron's dark picture of human waste is in effect, therefore, a beacon for progress. Grief has been conquered; so we are left not with bitterness but with an insistence that we assume freedom and responsibility as basic conditions of life, accept defeat and suffering—the full tragic conditions of life. Still we must try to create a purpose to offset the empty malice of a Moby Dick or the black edifice of Auschwitz. Otherwise, life would be neither bearable nor significant.

In his inaugural address, delivered in January 1989, President Bush discussed the final legacy of the Vietnam War, declaring, "No great nation can afford to be sundered by a memory." In effect, Bush urged national amnesia to encourage optimism and unity, rejecting the wisdom that is woe, thereby denying the possibility of awareness, repair, action, and personal meaning. Is this so very different from the German revisionist historians who claim that the Holocaust never happened, or from the Chinese government's attempt to deny its massacre of students in Tiananmen Square, claiming, while resodding the Square, that it merely "calmed" a "counterrevolutionary disturbance"? Bush's declaration is potentially as dangerous as Morris Fink's 1947 question, "What's Oswitch?" Clearly, there is still a need for Emersonian optimism in the America of the 1980s which betrays an unawareness of evil and ignorance of history similar to the America Melville confronted in the 1840s when he began his own exploration into our heart of darkness.

Sophie's Choice reminds us, however, that absolute evil will remain forever mysterious and inextinguishable and that Americans are not exempt from evil's lure; that is the meaning of Stingo's spiritual voyage. While it is obviously too late for Nathan and Sophie, Styron dramatizes through Stingo that the only way to confront Nazi inhumanity in retrospect is to show that it failed to dehumanize the judgment of its survivors.

5

Conclusion

Most of Styron's fiction examines the catastrophic propensity of human beings, either individually or collectively, to dominate others. As an artist, Styron is interested in "the anthropological make-up of humankind which makes war an apparently necessary activity" (Crane 20). The only solution to this propensity is to be able to imagine the plight of the recipients of our actions. "If we humans could look down the barrels, figurative or literal, of the guns we are prepared to fire, we surely would not shoot them. We would feel fear at least, perhaps even guilt" (Crane 30). While Styron acknowledges that we can never reach the firm conviction that we understand the Holocaust, neither can we withdraw from it in silence; silence can be interpreted as indifference. To an author concerned with the Holocaust, there seems little choice but to attempt to communicate the incommunicable.

At bottom, evil is unintelligible. Styron, then, is in a position not unlike Sisyphus; he cannot succeed in getting the rock to the top of the hill but neither can he give up the attempt. The majority of artists and philosophers have chosen silence in the face of the enormity of the horror, and many of Styron's critics have chided him for not remaining silent. Styron, however, would agree with Emil Fackenheim, Canadian theologian, philosopher, and religious existentialist: "The truth ... is that to grasp the Holocaust whole-of-horror is not to comprehend or transcend it, but rather to say no to it, or resist it" (Fackenheim 239). The real question to ask is not "Why did it happen?" but "Having seen what happened, what do we do now?"

Writing itself must do more than bear witness to horror; Melville, Camus, and Styron are writers whose works are, in effect, acts of metaphysical rebellion, acts of resistance against our evil potential. The humanistic task for Styron is to "defend the values which the Nazis denied their victims—to explain what respect for human life requires of us" (Seeskin 120). Styron's goal is clearly to raise our consciousness, but he knows his efforts will not miraculously change the world or eliminate evil. The post-

!ocaust years, the 1940s to the 1970s, were referred to as "wretched unending years of madness, illusion, error, dream, and strife" by the older, more mature voice of Styron's stand-in, Stingo.

A work of art, however, can be prophetic, generative. We can be restored only by fully confronting and somehow mastering the fact of absolute evil. In writing *Sophie's Choice,* Styron sought "the essential region of the soul where absolute evil confronts brotherhood." *Sophie's Choice* does force us to look into the abyss, but we can return with the wisdom that is woe. With awareness comes the potential for action, and with the action comes personal meaning.

Clearly, Styron has become engagé, marrying art to politics, which is not to say that he is a polemical writer. He writes for the "joy of creation, the joy that arises from the fulfillment of a need to grasp something of the nature of existence and set it down on paper" (Caputo 140). His novels resemble the work of Mann, Malraux, and Camus more than they do contemporary American writers. History, for Styron, is a "marvelous and clear mirror of human behavior" (Caputo 150).

In *The Confessions of Nat Turner* and *Sophie's Choice,* Styron has meditated on history, has recreated it by way of his personal conception of it. In the process, he offers the survivors of the Holocaust and other atrocities a kind of redemption through art. As critic Dawn Trouard contends:

> For Styron, the art of fiction and the art of history are co-extensive occupations which achieve meaning only when they are imaginatively realized and personally felt. The author forces himself into an interstice between event and recreation, thereby making meaning personal, even though mediated by the author's self-conscious presence. Through this risky juncture Styron offers aesthetic redemption for historical tragedy. (496)

Thanks to the honesty of *Sophie's Choice,* its bravery, and its good humor, it is a book that repairs the very loss it laments. Literature, then, can do more than simply bear witness to pain; it can help transcend the pain.

A testament to the power of *Sophie's Choice* is the fact that the novel until recently had been banned in South Africa, and only a heavily edited version will be available in the Soviet Union. It has also been banned in Poland because of its unflinching portrait of Polish anti-Semitism; there was to be a Polish underground edition of the novel, but with the newly elected, more liberal government, an underground edition will no longer be necessary. There have been over twenty foreign language editions of *Sophie's Choice.* Silence is obviously not the answer; writing about the horrors of war, the horrors of the Holocaust, does not trivialize them. The only way to trivialize war is to forget it, to ignore it.

A recent play in London claimed that the Holocaust was a conspiracy between Nazis and Zionists. A far-right candidate for the French presidency recently dismissed the Nazi gas chambers as a "footnote" to World War II history. The Austrians, under Kurt Waldheim, are reevaluating whether they were victims or accomplices of the Nazis, having commemorated the fiftieth anniversary of the Anschluss. The Poles had to defy a government ban to commemorate the 1943 Warsaw Ghetto Uprising. If we go in for silence, the Holocaust will be forgotten, and if it looms larger on the historical horizon than other atrocities, it will be because of literary treatments of it.

An interview I conducted with William Styron on May 4, 1988, at his home in Roxbury, Connecticut, is included in its entirety in an appendix. Because the questions were asked in the same order as the ideas raised in this book on *Sophie's Choice,* the interview can be read as a running commentary on those ideas.

The French honored Styron by awarding him the medal of the Commander of the Legion of Honor in 1984, the highest honor the French government bestows. It is hoped that Styron's winning the 1988 Edward MacDowell Medal for lifetime achievement and his being elected to the American Academy of Arts and Letters, the fifty-member inner body of the American Academy and Institute of Arts and Letters, will signal the beginning of American recognition of Styron's commanding contribution to twentieth-century literature; Styron's receiving the Nobel Prize would clearly be, for many, the right choice.

Appendix

A Conversation with William Styron

The author conducted this interview with William Styron at Styron's home in Roxbury, Connecticut, on 4 May 1989.

RS   In reviewing Robert Lifton's book, *The Nazi Doctors,* Bruno Bettelheim said trying to understand the vile Nazi doctors is wrong "because of the ever-present danger that understanding fully may come close to forgiving." There seems to be a conflict, then, between the need to recount or bear witness and the fear that understanding the Nazis comes close to forgiving them. How do you feel about this?

WS   I have great respect for Bruno Bettelheim, but I don't understand that kind of reasoning. I know Lifton's work, and I think the last thing he's attempting to do is to get people off the hook. He's trying to understand them. One of the absurdities behind capital punishment is, it seems to me, totally besides the immorality, is that if you destroy these people you miss the chance to study them. This is an extreme example, but basically the idea of taking a bunch of lunatics, who may not be so lunatic at all, as these doctors to try to discover what really made them perform these bestial acts makes sense. It seems ridiculous to think you shouldn't try to examine them.

RS   Is it inevitable to reduce the Holocaust, as one critic put it, "lose the Holocaust through metaphor" if you fictionalize it?

WS   I did it, obviously, and I think it's evident just from what I was trying to do that I thought anything but that. It's quite the opposite. That to fictionalize it or to try to understand it is kind of a mandate if you feel that's what you have to do.

RS   To understand horror must an artist portray it obliquely?

WS   Yes, and for that very reason I took the strategy I did, not to jump in and try to describe it from the point of view of a Jewish victim who had come from the Ukraine or someone who was there, but from the point of view of a young Southern boy who learns it from unpeeling many layers of a secret.

RS   So *Sophie's Choice* is not so much about the Holocaust but about discovering evil from uniquely American innocent eyes.

WS   Yes, indeed.

RS   One critic has accused you of capitalizing on the Holocaust fad, trivializing the Holocaust by ignoring the interconnection between the destiny of Judaism and the fate of Western civilization, linking you to revisionists who try to falsify or deny history.

WS   Which critic?

RS   Alan Berger, head of the Jewish Studies Department at Syracuse University.

WS   Does he link me to the people that say that the Holocaust did not exist? All I can say is that he's a nut. It wasn't my intention to deal with the destiny of Judaism. I was trying to write about a particular victim, in this case a hapless Gentile victim, of which there were, I might add, several million, and I find it obscene when people like that try to eliminate those people. In fact, if I ever wanted to mount a counterattack against any of these people whom I have heard about, whom I have never really read but whose words I have gotten rumors of, I would call them vicious. I would call them the betrayers of history who wilfully ignore the fact that for instance at Auschwitz alone there were a million and a half Poles who died, some of them in the gas chambers, but others who died as miserably as the Jews on a daily basis. Of course there was preferential treatment afforded to them and of course there are gradations, but a dead man is a dead man and dead woman is a dead woman. It doesn't matter what race you are or whether you are circumcized or not.

RS   A convention held a year ago in Albany called "Writing and the Holocaust" seemed to be geared to the Holocaust as a Jewish phenomenon. One man from the audience, however, screamed at some panelists, "Are you aware that Hitler not only disliked the Jews but that he was not too fond of homosexuals either?" Writer and panelist Cynthia Ozick retorted, "How dare you compare the struggle of the Jews with homosexuality."

WS   Yes, right. There you go. Terrific. I have always found that the intentional ignoring of the fate of a lot of other people has been one of the major moral derelictions of Jewish thinkers on the subject. There have been some brave Jewish activists, people like Simon Wiesenthal, who have always said that we must remember that there were other victims and has constantly pointed out that it is dangerous to take unto themselves this exclusivity and to say that there were no other victims because he said this is going to redound to the discredit of the Jews eventually. This is from Simon Wiesenthal.

RS The two central arguments against your having written this novel are that you are not a survivor or Jewish yourself and that nobody should fictionalize the Holocaust. Should artists always be granted their donnée, their subject?

WS If this were true, we would have no art, no fiction. If I had to be a survivor of Auschwitz, there is no possible way I could approach it. One of the key virtues of the literary method, of literary art, is its ability, its impetus, to try to do anything, to go for broke, for a man to write like a woman, or for a woman to write like a man, to jump racial barriers, to jump sex and sexual barriers. The idea that I would have to be a victim of the Holocaust to write about it is absurd as is its corollary about fictionalizing it. These are absurd questions not worthy of a great deal of discussion.

RS M. Scott Peck, psychoanalyst and author of *People of the Lie: The Hope for Healing Human Evil,* contends that we cannot heal that which we do not even dare study. Evil for him is a mysterious illness, and those who oppose the life force deserve more pity than hatred; evil originates not in the absence of guilt but in the effort to escape it. He feels you cannot conquer evil by destroying it; only through love is this possible.

WS I think that sounds like a strange vapor to me. I don't understand it. He's a local guru. I've never met him, but I don't think you can lay down any firm edicts on evil except to say that it exists and somehow it perpetuates itself and what can you do except try to expose it whenever you see it.

RS You certainly cannot wipe it out with one blow!

WS I think that sounds like a terrible platitude. Love is desirable, but I don't think love conquers all as the saying goes.

RS Are you familiar with the work of Alice Miller?

WS She's a psychoanalyst, Swiss?

RS Originally German. She has written three books in the 1980s exploring the roots of evil, violence, and madness. Her work was considered so seditious that she had to leave her native Germany to practice and write in Switzerland. She believes that human destructiveness is a reactive, not innate phenomenon, that every persecutor was once a victim, that the need to commit murder is the outcome of a tragic childhood. She indicts, therefore, any society which rears its children through physical force or humiliation claiming it is for their own good. How do you respond to her ideas?

WS   Well, I think she's got probably part of a truth, but I don't think it's anywhere near the whole truth. I think you can probably say that many people prone to violence have had miserable childhoods, but that this certainly is not true for all people. I think many homicidal murderers, maniacs so called, might have had perfectly happy childhoods. But I do think there is something to be said for this. Like all psychoanalysts she tends towards broad generalizations when she should be satisfied with plucking part of the truth.

RS   Alice Miller has a chapter in one of her books describing the daily beatings Hitler received from his father where his mother stands by and watches, and a chapter on the beatings Kafka received from his father.

WS   But Kafka didn't become a homicidal maniac. He became a great artist. So the battered can become potential artists and potential homicidal maniacs!

RS   *Sophie's Choice* can be read as an education novel where the education is in the enigma and pain of existence. Isn't this a way to gain some artistic distance from the Holocaust, which really can only be apprehended obliquely?

WS   Yes, I think there is some good perception in that in the sense that distance is the key word for me. I wanted very much to write about this whole experience, but I knew I dare not get into anything, and this is where some of the critics would be on the right track by saying how as a nonsurvivor I would be on very shaky ground if I tried to get myself into a situation where I was describing, let's say, Sophie from the point of view of her barracks experience, the whole bit—the beatings, the tortures, the humiliations, the deprivations, the freezing, the terrible roll calls—that if I did that I would be treading on very dangerous grounds. Just as I would have if writing about the black experience, about Negro slavery, trying to do something about the whole black experience. If I had, for instance, dared to write about blacks in Harlem, writing about another modern contemporary slavery, I would have been on totally fraudulent grounds because I would be totally out of my depth. So it is important to me to write about that experience from the vantage point of distance of a hundred and something years, one hundred and fifty years, between me and slavery, which gave me an authentic voice, just as authentic as a black man. The same with Sophie and her experience in the concentration camp. I wanted to get many distances. I wanted not only to distance myself as narrator from the situation but from Sophie. So the whole thing about Sophie is written from the vantage point of her experience outside the concentration camp. The closest she gets is in the Commandant's house, which is outside the compound. I wanted to portray the periphery of the experience so that one senses through the sounds the horror. That's what I intended to do. Some critics have seemed to understand that. Sophie smells the Jews being burned in the gas chambers. She hears the boxcars. She even hears the pistol shots. She hears the screams. This is a form of wanting to distance myself from the whole experience which was necessary and that is why, if the book works, and I think it does, it works because of this distance.

RS Do you agree that *Sophie's Choice* is a continuation of *Nat Turner?* Are both novels really about slavery?

WS Yes, definitely.

RS You make a parallel between the old South and what's going on in the camps.

WS Well, I didn't want to belabor the point, but I do think there are similarities. I do think that when I quoted Richard Rubenstein in the novel I was on the right track because I think he was on the right track. He was trying to point out that Auschwitz was also, although it was an extermination camp, a slave labor camp—the only real mass-scale modern slave labor we have had, an extension of the slavery of the nineteenth century.

RS In Hannah Arendt's still controversial book, *Eichmann in Jerusalem,* she maintains that Eichmann was not a monster but terrifyingly normal—a new type of criminal who can commit a crime without feeling that he is doing wrong. In order to commit genocide, the Nazis had to turn around their natural instincts of pity. Is this related to your portrait of Dr. von Niemand?

WS Yes. I think Hannah Arendt's insights were very sound. I understand again why people like Alvin Rosenfeld—probably the same people who would criticize her would criticize me—but I found her insights brilliant, and I think they are certainly related to von Niemand and the others in the book, to Rudolf Höss, a functionary. They found ways to rationalize the commission of evil. That was the most important thing.

RS You even compare Eichmann to Lieutenant Calley.

WS Somewhere, yes.

RS Were you thinking of the Old Testament prophet Nathan and Nat Turner when you created Nathan Landau?

WS   No, it's a coincidence.

RS   Do you think Nathan is suffering from his own form of survivor guilt?

WS   I'm not really sure. There might be a touch of that in his behavior.

RS   Would this not explain why he battered Sophie?

WS   Yes.

RS   In a book about your fiction Judith Ruderman contends that the Jews you have created are often moral touchstones, outsiders and rebels, not passive victims. Was that your intention?

WS   Yes, I think there might be some validity in that. I didn't consciously ordain that, but I think maybe that does bubble up to the surface.

RS   After all, Nathan is rebuking the world for murder!

WS   Yeah, right.

RS   *Sophie's Choice* has been criticized for its humor, some considering the comic scenes inappropriate in a novel about the Holocaust. But isn't the Jewish comic mode really an awareness of life's horror, a strategy adopted as a defense against tragedy?

WS   Yes. I think anyone who would attack the book on this ground is too solemn or dreary really to argue with. The point is the book is a novel. I tried to create a sense of life which mercifully contains humor, and if the book has humor, and it does, it has it because it's a slice of life. One of the things indeed as a countercriticism that has always bothered me about so much of the literature about the Holocaust is its total absence of humor. To be sure, it's a horrible subject, but no subject is so horrible that it doesn't have humor in it, and this has always bothered me about this approach. Nothing is so sacred that it doesn't have even a ripple of humor, black humor. I have several friends who are survivors of the worst battles of the Pacific War. Two observations I'd like to make about this. You can never equate Auschwitz with warfare. They are two different things. What I think I'm saying about warfare is that at its worst it's a terrible ordeal. It does allow you to talk about suffering in a very specific way. I guess I'm saying that what bothers me about certain aspects of the Holocaust is this kind of treasuring of virtue. I would not have written about it if I had not whole-heartedly agreed that it was one of the greatest moral horrors of human history, but to allow that to totally extinguish any other claim to suffering bothers me. I'm bothered because human suffering is not the property of any one person, any one group, any one experience. I am reminded of several years ago when I was bedeviled by a survivor of Auschwitz, a woman who wrote a book of memoirs, and she wanted me to give her comments. When I didn't, she wrote angry letters. I knew something about her. She had been a survivor. The book was a compendium of memories which really recapitulate a lot of the memories of the survivors, pretty standard stuff. I don't mean to depreciate it; it's horrible. I met her briefly in New York. She had married a broker here in the United States, and she was complaining although she had a diamond the size of a robin's egg and was extremely chicly dressed. Certainly physically she had emerged un-scathed though she plainly had psychic wounds of a survivor. But she bothered me because there was a certain self-righteousness about her. I had a different wartime experience. I was very lucky to survive the Pacific, but I had friends who were on Iwo Jima, and a friend was made a quadriplegic. He's been in a hospital ever since, immobile. I think he would say that he would rather have been a survivor or Auschwitz. This woman with her self-righteous view is like a lot of people who discuss the Holocaust as if it were something so sacrosanct that nothing can penetrate it. This I reject. My own moral sense tells me that I cannot accept this. Auschwitz was itself a horror of inconceivable dimensions. But I find morally reprehensible the idea that something about it is so sacrosanct that other people are not capable of trying to reexperience it or that there are other forms of suffering which are just as valid, just as horrible, and just as either noble or ignoble depending on the way you look at it. People are still to this day suffering from wounds of a different kind of war, but it's just as valid a fight against the forces of evil and deserves to be remembered. This atrocious lady with her robin's-egg diamond accusing me of some sort of dereliction!

RS Elie Wiesel dedicated his Nobel Prize in 1986 to the survivors for "teaching us how not to succumb to despair." Can't *Sophie's Choice* be read as attempting to do the same thing?

WS I think that's a good reading, and I'm glad you feel that way.

RS *Sophie's Choice* has engendered controversy as well for its frank sexu-ality. Some have called the novel pornographic or at least too preoccupied with sex in a novel supposedly about the Holocaust. The sexuality is seen, therefore, as inappropriate. How do you feel about this?

WS I gather this guy Rosenfeld made a great issue of that, the one who called the novel "the erotics of Auschwitz." In the first place, there are intertwining stories. There's Stingo's story. He is a sexually avid young man who is living a sexually avid life in which sex is an important part of his configuration. Why should I not write about it? That's my first answer.

RS   Some critics think the novel is Sophie's story and, therefore, question why you spend time on Stingo's sex life.

WS   It's about Stingo as well, about his reactions to things. The chief counterargument I have to the idea that I have made pornographic the actual Auschwitz part is that if I had wanted to be pornographic or even subpornographic but titillating I would have had a scene in which instead of the Commandant grappling with Sophie he would have been in bed with her, and I would have described him fucking her. It would have been very easy to do. I could have done it. But I didn't. The second point I'd like to make about that is that eroticism as I gather in reading material about Auschwitz was almost a barometer of health. That is, when people were suffering, eroticism played no part whatsoever, which is true as it is in sickness, personal sickness. The first thing to disappear is sexual desire. But there was a great deal of erotic activity going on around the camps just as there was during slave times, just as there was in all human activities and especially when the activity involves power. Women were bought and sold at Auschwitz. The Commandant was a well-known eyer of good-looking women. That is an actual fact.

RS   Aryan only?

WS   Any kind. The ethnic thing was absolutely dissolved. So many accounts I've read of other Nazis indicate that when a good-looking Jewish gal came along, she was fair game. The idea of their so-called inferiority meant nothing. What I am trying to say is eroticism, being part of life, never faded. At Auschwitz, as a matter of fact, it often took a rather vigorous form because of the power. So to ignore it and leave it out of the picture would have been, it seems to me, as absurd as overemphasizing it.

RS   I think some critics were more upset with all of Stingo's fantasies and autoeroticism.

WS   Why?

RS   Because it was inappropriate in a novel about the Holocaust—but is it just a novel about the Holocaust?

WS   I leaned over backwards to give an open-ended view of things. I wanted to make this a young man's story so that you would know that young man, so that in turn when the young man began to learn about Auschwitz, you would have this filtered through a young man's consciousness. A young man is full of erotic thoughts. It's part of his daily life. To have ignored that would have made him a very weird young man, especially in those days. When a young man is not getting laid, he masturbates, even when he is getting laid. So the idea that autoerotic thoughts would be absent from the narrative would be puritanical.

RS   Ironically, you attack our puritanical values in the novel and call America of the 1940s a "nightmarish Sargasso Sea of guilts and apprehension."

WS   Exactly.

RS   The novel has also been called sexist. Some critics indict Stingo's limited male perspective which doesn't allow Sophie to speak for herself. Would it not be more accurate to say that the novel explores sexism without itself being sexist?

WS   Yes. I don't understand any charge against the book on sexist lines. This is Gloria Steinem's view. I refuse to countenance any kind of criticism of a book which is so political. The politics of sex is so intense as to prevent the writer from creating the character in any way he wants to. I have created a woman who is used, among other things, by men.

RS   Some feminists argue that you tend to create weak, dependent, deceitful, suicidal women, that this indicates misogyny either on your part or on the male narrator's part. On the other hand, some critics claim that you have created women with tragic stature, Peyton Loftis and Sophie. How do you explain this split?

WS   Well, Gloria Steinem is not a literary critic. She's a politician and a propagandist. She wants cardboard women who would fall into her view of noble, long-suffering, but triumphant women. She's basically not very bright. She's a preposterous woman. I think she's done some good things on her own, but she should leave literary criticism to other people.

RS   Some see Stingo as the villain of the novel, exploiting Sophie's story for material, as an unreliable narrator, basically narcissistic and egotistical.

WS   The point is he might be narcissistic and egotistical. I find it interesting that people would impute to narcissism some kind of evil. Many people are narcissistic. He's egotistical, perhaps. What's wrong with that?

RS   He's also twenty-two.

WS   Yes. Suppose he were the opposite of egotistical which is a wimp, a self-flagellating wimp. Would they prefer that? The point is you have to create somebody who is something. If it involves narcissism and ego, so what?

RS   Part of the argument against Stingo as narrator is that because he is so sexually turned on by Sophie, he cannot relate her story honestly.

WS   I don't understand the flaw there because I don't understand what it is she would tell him that would be altered by a more objective view rather than his. He is sexually attracted to her, but I don't see how this interferes with the story.

RS   You mean it doesn't diminish her anguish because he is attracted to her.

WS   That's right.

RS   Why does Sophie choose to have Eva murdered rather than Jan?

WS   Suppose she had Jan instead of Eva murdered. Would it be all right for a male chauvinist to say that she had made the wrong selection?

RS   There is no right selection.

WS   There is no right selection. How could this be? It's absurd.

RS   At a recent children of survivors meeting, the novel came up, and I was told that some women criticized you for giving Sophie the "luxury" of a choice.

WS   I think people who feel that simply have missed the point of the book entirely.

RS   Female self-hatred is shown to be a result of a fiercely patriarchal culture which is not to say that masochism is innate to women, which Steinem claims you feel.

WS   I don't say that. There is where I just throw up my hands because it's as if by creating a woman like Sophie in the eyes of Gloria Steinem I'm creating an archetype. I'm creating an individual woman. She may have been masochistic. Many women are masochistic. She wanted me to create an archetype which you don't do in a novel. It's preposterous.

RS   One can counter Steinem's view by giving good reasons why Stingo is the perfect sympathetic narrator for Sophie's story: both Stingo and Sophie suffer from their own forms of survivor guilt; they are both Gentile; they are both dazzled by the same man; they share guilt over the genocidal past of their countries; and they must confront stereotypes of Jews and blacks.

WS   I think that's a fair assumption. That holds.

RS   Is there not a profound psychological connection between Stingo and Sophie? They both dream about their opposite sex parent and are both orphans in a way. Their dreams reveal the human tendency to punish oneself for unpreventable deaths. Stingo stops idealizing his parents, no longer desperate for approval. Isn't that partially what saves him and destroys Sophie?

WS   Yes. There's an imperative for her that is different.

RS   Sophie's unhealthy attachment is graphically contrasted with Stingo's healthy attachment to a sympathetic father. Is Sophie's fate, then, largely her father's responsibility?

WS   Well, I would say that in the symbolic scheme of things, as I said before, the fact that this man was a rabid anti-Semite metaphorically sealed her doom. It was his collusion with the Nazis that more or less was symbolic of the doom that he really wished upon Jews but which involved Sophie and his grandchildren. So her fate was connected to her father's.

RS   It was not only her father's rabid anti-Semitism, but it seems to me the whole sexist culture. Her mother was described as a sweet, self-effacing woman. Sophie is told that she is stupid; she dreams about her father's taking the piano away from her. There is that sense that she cannot be who she is partially because her father won't let her.

WS   Excellent. It must have driven Gloria Steinem crazy for me not to have created some other kind of father, so that I would have fallen under her rubric of creating everything that was disadvantageous to women. Sophie is almost an archetypal figure of the female who is beset upon by every male she meets: her father, husband, lover, the Commandant, Dürrfeld. Every male that she has any relationship with has a ruthless, dominant, destructive connection with her.

RS   Not that masochism is innate. That's not the point. But it is a problem that she doesn't have another role model.

WS   She doesn't. But the point is that she can't be all things to all women. She is who she is. The point is, too, that totally aside from this, Gloria Steinem is an ignoramus. She fails to realize this. I've had several Polish women tell me they are impressed by the accuracy of my portrait of this particular kind of culture she came from—a male-dominant, Catholic, judgmental, dominating culture—what Poland was between the wars. Sophie is the perfect by-product of this culture. Too bad Gloria Steinem finds this, well, somebody should tell her she's ignorant, she's dumb.

RS   Doesn't Stingo have to learn that it is not his responsibility to rescue or save women, that manhood means a lot more than sexual conquest and gratification?

WS   Yes, indeed.

RS   Many have linked Stingo's Oedipal problems, his failure to save his mother, to his troubles with women.

WS   Yes, but he's twenty-two, and he learns that after he has sexual gratification.

RS   Some have criticized the inclusion of the Leslie Lapidus and Mary Alice Grimball material, but isn't the novel at least partially about sexual repression which can lead to perversity? Isn't it a terrible irony, then, that the film version of the novel was so sexually timid?

WS   I couldn't agree with you more. When the movie premiered in Paris, I was asked to go over there, and a French journalist asked me just that question. They all read the book, and they said, "Where's the sex?" The eroticism is not there. I think Pakula, the director, did some very fine things in the movie. It was a superior movie, but he really missed the ball when it came to sexuality.

RS   Do you think it was that he wanted to whitewash it a little so that it would play all over the country?

WS   Well, it was R-Rated anyway. I don't think he is a very sexy director.

RS   The sexuality among the three of them just is not there.

WS   No, it's not. Because it's so urgent and alive, the three of them come within a hair of going to bed with each other. They don't, but it verges on that, on being a ménage à trois.

RS   I think the problem was with the casting. Peter MacNicol just looked like sixteen.

WS   Agreed. There are occasional girls who are turned on by young men, but he is just too young. He's fine for Nathan if Nathan were that way, which he just isn't, but I think it was a bad piece of miscasting. It made him too callow among other things. He had that Gomer Pyle accent. They had a chance to get Timothy Hutton for the part.

RS   How do you feel about the exclusion of the sexual scenes in the Russian translation of the novel?

WS   I had to do that because they can't even under Gorbachev, I gather. I had to go sit down with the translator while she would take things out of the English version. She laughed when she said, "This is unlawful in our country." She had to excise all the sexual scenes—the Mary Alice material, Stingo's fantasies, the final sex scene between Stingo and Sophie.

RS   What was her attitude about expurgating the text?

WS· She was regretful. She said it was unlawful. She said I hate to do this. We had a long discussion about this. She said the sexual urgency of his desires throughout the book in general and specifically with Sophie were so intense that it's perfectly natural to have this finally happen. It's dramatically the right place for it. It's just the way it should be done. She said I'm personally not the slightest bothered by the explicitness, but I cannot translate it into Russian. So we were both regretful. There are critics who are in favor of no explicit sexual details in novels. We can always go back to Tolstoy and *Anna Karenina*. The famous scene where Vronsky goes to bed with Anna and then there's this space. How ironic that is. He could so easily have written explicitly about this. He would have done a terrific job. I can imagine what he would have done. It would have been unbelievable. Think what if Tolstoy were given, which he wasn't because it was unlawful then too, well, he would have done it explicitly, but he would have done it with style and grace, and it would have been wonderful. It's like Robert Coover's wonderful piece not long ago in one of the magazines which was later collected in book form of "Casablanca" with Rick and whatever her name was and spins this wonderful pornographic fantasy of what they actually did in bed.

RS   You mean what they left out of the movie?

WS   Yes.

RS   You link religious and sexual repression in your novel. The one sexual union between Stingo and Sophie is couched in religious terminology. Are you suggesting that joyous lovemaking is the closest we are ever to get to salvation?

WS   What religious terminology?

RS   Prayer, God, ecstasy.

WS   It's one of the fulfillments that is as valid as the religious experience, I being a cynic about religion. I think you could say that it's on a plane with the religious experience if it's not something in itself that is overidealized. It's only been in recent years, in our time, that sexuality is accepted in the Western experience and not other cultures as something that is good in itself. It's not an adjunct to something. It has its own reason for being, its own desirability as a pursuit which is as valid to me as religion.

RS   I think Stingo calls it a pursuit of "good, wholesome, heterosexual screwing."

WS   Yes. Some critic rather poignantly or graphically pointed out in his review that when Sophie died, Stingo's sperm was inside of her, for what it's worth. This complicates the view. But I actually read a commentary like this.

RS   To what end? What does this illustrate?

WS   That somehow he had usurped Nathan's role as lover.

RS   The point is that she and Nathan are dead.

WS   Exactly.

RS   There is a link between political and sexual brutality in the novel. Are we not meant to contrast the routine, legitimized, efficient sadism of the camps with Nathan's madness-induced, irrational sadism?

WS   Sure.

RS   You call sex in mid-twentieth-century America a "nightmarish Sargasso Sea of guilts and apprehension." Has much changed since World War II in this country regarding our sexual attitudes?

WS   Yes. There was a great revolution after that and things became much more open. I do think the late 30s, 40s, and 50s were times of extreme rigorous conventionality. No doubt about it. Girls got married, M-A-R-R-I-E-D. Boys were expected to be husbands, H-U-S-B-A-N-D-S. Then there was this extraordinary explosion. Things certainly did change for the better although the United States is still basically a puritanical country. For instance, this whole thing about Gary Hart. Many of my French friends said Gary Hart would have been elected instantly.

RS   Besides being Sophie's final torturer, can't we say that it is Nathan who brings out Sophie's innate sexuality and sensuality? While there is a good deal of sexual lunacy between the two of them, is there not a model presented of "good, wholesome heterosexual screwing" as contrasted with Stingo's encounters with American women?

WS   Sure. Because she lived this Polish life of buried eroticism. It didn't exist in her.

RS   Her husband and lover are either impotent or dysfunctional.

WS   Yes. And as I said, Nathan, I implied, was the first person to make her come. This was something she had never experienced with this ghastly husband that she had. She was just abandoned with this guy.

RS   Not to mention oral sex. She only fantasized about this in Poland.

WS   That's right. Then all of a sudden she could do it with Nathan.

RS   Patterns of sexuality are shown, then, to be historically and culturally determined. You link Polish Catholic repression, Southern Presbyterian repression, and Flatbush Jewish repression.

WS   There's no doubt about it. Sexuality is culturally determined. I'm convinced. Why should Gary Hart cause such a terrible stir here? In France, there's a tradition of leaders, of which Gary Hart aspired to; they had a whole tradition developed through feudalism of these leaders having affairs. There was never a French king who didn't have a whole slew of bastard children, perfectly approved, largely because of the connection between the man and his various girls who may have been servants or courtiers or whatever, but we don't have that tradition. We have a tradition of purity and monogamy, and Gary Hart didn't fall into that category. You're absolutely right. Sexuality is culturally determined.

RS   What one feels very often in your novels is the "merciless and ugly face of loneliness." Sex is rarely a form of intimate connection in your novels.

WS   Maybe, but sex is a desirable outcome, and I have tried, much of this unconsciously, to show that the moments of sex between Nathan and Sophie were these extraordinary apotheoses, these grand moments, and this was a demonstration of some degree of the life force you mentioned, even though they were doomed because of his instability and her own doom herself.

RS   Sex is in some ways the symbolic setting of *Sophie's Choice*—the Sargasso Sea of post-Holocaust moral confusion. Would you agree? After all, Stingo is as confused about sexuality as Leslie Lapidus and Mary Alice Grimball.

WS   Yes. It's a moral confusion because the priorities and the balances in society are off. You can't live in a society which in all of its media presentations celebrates sex and then prohibits it. As I have pointed out, automobiles were developed with larger back seats for horizontal fornication, but there was still this prohibition. This imposes a terrific tension and a very pernicious tension on both males and females, and that's part of the moral confusion.

RS   While some of the sexual scenes are very funny, the sexual problem between the sexes is taken very seriously in the novel.

WS   Exactly right.

RS   Some critics have placed your novel in the Southern Gothic tradition, a tradition where the protagonist awakes from a nightmare vision. Do you share this view?

WS   This is somebody's dumb idea. There is nothing particularly Southern or Gothic about the novel, except that the narrator happens to come from the South.

RS   Pauline Kael of *The New Yorker* calls *Sophie's Choice* your "Holocaust Gothic."

WS   I love the idea of a movie critic suddenly becoming a literary critic!

RS   I see many Melvillean overtones in *Sophie's Choice*. You have mentioned that Melville is one of your favorite novelists. Other than beginning your novel with "Call me Stingo," were there other connections to *Moby-Dick* in terms of characters, theme, action, and overall architecture?

WS   I don't really know. It's hard for me to say when I'm that close to a book. It's hard for me to extrapolate. When it comes to literary influence, that's more or less your job, not mine.

RS   Perhaps I could offer a few parallels and you could tell me whether you feel they are accurate.

WS   Fine.

RS   I see *Moby-Dick* and *Sophie's Choice* as metaphysical voyages into the mysteries of evil, madness, love, and death. Both Ishmael and Stingo are rebellious voyagers essentially writing spiritual autobiographies. The problem of evil haunts both novels, spawning a moral quest, a search for values.

WS   Yes, that's close. It's a good point.

RS   Melville was an anti-Transcendentalist. He refused to accept Emerson's notion that evil was just the privation of good. In so doing, Melville rebuked Emerson's and America's empty optimism of the 1840s, a century before the setting of *Sophie's Choice*. Doesn't your novel rebuke America for the same mindless and boundless optimism which actually betrays an unawareness of evil and ignorance of history?

WS   Melville was right. I think there's a continuity there. I'll buy that.

RS   So you're in the tradition of Hawthorne and Melville.

WS   That's all right with me.

RS   You and Melville also share a close personal link to slavery. Your grandmother owned slaves, and Melville's father-in-law, Judge Lemuel Shaw, was the first Northern judge to enforce the rigorous Fugitive Slave Laws penalizing those helping runaway slaves. He also upheld segregated schooling in Boston. Melville saw slavery as the betrayal of the American

Revolution's egalitarian ideals. Race features prominently in Melville's fiction as well as yours.

WS   Yes, there's a close personal link. There's a connection. These things you have conceived I can only nod at, assent, and say yes. I can't say yes or no, but I can feel the connection.

RS   Would it be fair to say that Melville and you share not only a consciousness of racial division but a belief that interracial harmony must not be just an abstract ideal but is necessary for human survival?

WS   Interracial harmony, certainly. Whether we will ever achieve racial integration is something else, but total integration I think is impossible. But harmony has to be achieved, yes.

RS   Would you say the resurrections at the end of both novels are humanistic and not religious?

WS   Yes, quite sure. They are not religious.

RS   Besides Ishmael and Stingo, there are interesting parallels between Ahab and Nathan, both outraged by evil's power and capriciousness. Their spiritual revolts, however, take on a murderous edge. Both are destroyed by the knowledge of demonism in the world. Aren't Ahab and Nathan both fatally glamorous?

WS   I would like to think so.

RS   Both Ahab and Nathan have the woe that is madness. Even though they push their quests too far, aren't their "spear-hurling" gestures admirable and necessary in an iniquitous world?

WS   I think that they are both flamboyant and basically attractive figures even though they have unattractive, negative qualities.

RS   Nathan and Ahab have achieved what Melville calls the woe that is madness, but Stingo and Ishmael have achieved the wisdom that is woe which helps them survive.

WS   Good point. You're doing very well.

RS   Pip and Sophie also have the woe that is madness, both dealt blows from which they are unable to recover; both see the heartless immensity of the universe which drowns the infinite of their souls, to quote Melville. Stingo and Ishmael, however, are able to conquer their grief, which explains their survival.

WS   Yes, I'll buy that.

RS Pip and Sophie are victims of racial madness. Their suffering takes a passive form. Dwelling too much on the horrors of existence can take active forms as well, as in the cases of Ahab and Nathan. They feel they can eliminate evil but create evil in the process. Is this not connected to the zealotry of Sophie's father and Nat Turner?

WS Yes, I see a connection.

RS Neither you nor Melville offers religious consolation. The resurrections at the end of your novels are accidental. It is Ishmael's friendship with Queequeg which literally buoys him, and it is the instinctive compassion from children at Coney Island which saves Stingo. Would you agree that you and Melville both demonstrate the importance of human solidarity in a world in which we are all strangers abandoned in an indifferent, meaningless universe?

WS I'll go for that. I see the connections. You are making interesting connections, and I am appreciative of the expansiveness of your views.

RS Would you agree that *Moby-Dick* and *Sophie's Choice* are anti-Christian novels, the former a revolt against a cruel cosmos, the latter a revolt against human tyranny, human evil?

WS Yes, absolutely.

RS One of your early influences was Conrad. Did his novella *Heart of Darkness* influence your work?

WS Only insofar as Conrad saturated my thoughts. I don't think that I would make any direct connection. This was not conscious, but Conrad was a helpful influence on my work. I'll go that far.

RS Kurtz is, after all, like Nathan, destroyed by demonism, and Marlow comes as close to the abyss as possible, like Stingo.

WS Quite so.

RS Your book of essays, *This Quiet Dust,* was compared by critic Melvin Friedman to Camus' collected essays. The reviews, however, were lukewarm.

WS Well, it's not that good. It's hard to do anything in this country without getting shot down.

RS This is the perfect segue to Camus. In many ways you are more European than American.

WS That's why I think I'm pretty well appreciated in Europe, more so than here, in a curious way.

RS   *Sophie's Choice* is considered one of the most significant novels to have emerged since the Second World War in France. Not so in this country.

WS   Certainly not.

RS   What European existentialists influenced your work?

WS   Malraux, philosophically. Sartre, Camus definitely. I began to read the writers that they read—Heidegger and Kierkegaard—and gained quite a bit from them.

RS   Do you know Camus' favorite American novel?

WS   No.

RS   *Moby-Dick*. He called it a truly absurd work.

WS   Now that you mention it, I did realize that.

RS   Would you agree with Camus about the dangers of believing in absolutes.

WS   You bet. You very well bet because that's the true danger.

RS   While Camus warns us of the danger of believing in nothing, nihilism, isn't it equally dangerous to argue that evil is just the privation of good?

WS   Indeed. I can't buy Emerson's notion.

RS   Americans are still affected by Emerson's often childish views.

WS   I'm afraid so.

RS   Would you agree with Camus that the novel must be the literature of rebellion, not consent?

WS   I think insofar as I feel allied spiritually to Camus because of that dark, heavy strain of rebelliousness, I feel I share that in my work, that rebellion.

RS   The first chapter of *Sophie's Choice* was criticized as being too digressive. But Stingo's rebellious nature is demonstrated in that opening chapter.

WS   The point is that when people say that, I tend to shrug or turn away because the whole first chapter of *Moby-Dick* has nothing itself to do with the issue at hand. It's just there. Queequeg, the bed, the slightly homosexual overtone which is delightful to read. But the whole chapter could go out in terms of the architecture of the book and would not be injurious. But it is preferable that it stays in. It has nothing to do with the whaling part, the voyage itself. It's preliminary.

RS   But the chapter is integral in the sense that it establishes character, a disaffected schoolteacher who is feeling suicidal and decides to take to the sea.

WS   It does establish character, and that's a key phrase, the one you just used. Half the weight of the first chapter of *Sophie's Choice* is to let the reader know that he's in the hands of someone who has had this kind of experience, a disaffected young man with a certain mindset, who is rebellious to a certain degree. Without all that, you wouldn't understand what's going to happen when he meets Sophie and Nathan in Brooklyn.

RS   The whole system of oppression gets set up in the beginning of the novel, so it's not a digression.

WS   Only an academic critic at his worst would criticize the opening chapter as too digressive. I know that *Sophie's Choice* is filled with irrelevancies in terms of absolute architechtonic perfection. I knew that when I was writing it. All sorts of digressions. But look at *Moby-Dick*. Who cares. If you don't want digressions, read another book.

RS   The Leslie Lapidus and Mary Alice Grimball scenes have also been called digressions, but since sexuality is so germane to the novel, these scenes are not truly digressive.

WS   Yes, right.

RS   As opposed to a lot of minimalist fiction today, the old novels used to position themselves against alienation, loneliness, and industrialization. Novelists were speakers, not just alienated spectators. Isn't it important, therefore, that Stingo is not mere spectator but participant in the action?

WS   Yes. Except for the concentration camp scenes, he's there except for when Sophie's mind takes over and becomes the narrative voice. Stingo's voice is omnipresent.

RS   Again, that's similar to Melville. Both of you feel that alienation very acutely and struggle against it. Stingo and Bartleby struggle against the world of big business, that "soulless empire" as you put it.

WS   Exactly so.

RS   In your fiction and nonfiction you have shown what happens when an individual lacks guilt or remorse. The Commandant is an obvious example, and you have written about Lieutenant Calley, an Eichmann-like figure. On the other hand, you present Jozef, the young Resistance fighter, who vomits and is nearly driven insane when he is forced to kill an informer, and Dr. von Niemand, who bridges the two sides in a way. To be fully human is to feel guilt. How do you explain this lack of remorse, the inability to own up to one's transgressions and take the punishment? I'm thinking of recent examples like Robert McFarlane, Michael Deaver, Lyn Nofziger, Oliver North, and others.

WS   Good point. That's a very good cross-connection. The ones you mentioned, leave Deaver out because he's a pathetic nonentity, are really zealots who believe that what they did was right and that, therefore, they can't be shaken into guilt because they feel they have no guilt to acknowledge, especially true of North.

RS   I hear North wants to run for Senator from Virginia.

WS   The perfect state for it, my native state. The most reactionary state in the Union, more than Mississippi. The perfect state. I'm being parenthetical here. I don't know if you saw it, but I testified against Judge Bork, and I want to make a connection. I got a telegram a few days ago, and I want to show it to you. This is May, and I testified in September. The man who sent me the telegram tells me that I am no longer a Virginian, no longer a son of the old dominion. That's an indication of the mentality of the typical Virginia urban reactionary. Can you imagine him brooding over this testimony so many months that he would finally decide to send me this telegram!

RS   You keep all these things?

WS   Yes. That's an indication of North and the state of Virginia. I don't know whether he would win or not, but it's a serious bid.

RS   Hardy said, "If a way to the Better there be, it exacts a full look at the worst." American naturalists of the late nineteenth and early twentieth century believed that. There was, then, a reformist or idealist strain in some naturalist fiction. Do you see much American fiction which retains this reformist or idealist strain today?

WS   No, but those who do are preaching to the already converted.

RS   The madness of the Nazi era is still with us. Austria elects Waldheim while reevaluating whether it was an accomplice of the Nazis or its victim during its fiftieth anniversary of the Anschluss; the Polish people have to defy a government ban to commemorate the 1943 Warsaw Ghetto Uprising; and Demyanyuk is sentenced to be hanged in Israel. War does not seem to be a temporary madness as Melville put it, but the human condition in the twentieth century.

WS   Alas. Quite so.

RS Is the only solution to war, slavery, suffering being able to imagine the plight of the victim, to "look down the barrel of your own gun," as critic John Crane puts it?

WS There must be an identification with the victim, yes.

RS Joseph Brodsky, recent winner of the Nobel Prize for literature, said that future political leaders should be asked not about foreign policy first but about their attitudes towards Stendhal, Dickens, and Dostoevsky. He feels that if we chose our leaders according to their reading and not their political programs there would be less grief. Do you agree?

WS Of course Brodsky is being too idealistic here, but there is something to this. I am personally embarrassed to live in a country that has an actor for its president. Can you imagine Reagan reading Stendhal, Dickens, or Dostoevsky!

RS Finally, perhaps you could discuss your current work a bit. Are you continuing your work on *A Tidewater Morning,* an excerpt of which originally appeared in *Esquire* magazine in August 1987? Will you continue working on *The Way of the Warrior,* the novel you left to write *Sophie's Choice?*

WS I prefer not discussing my current work in any detail, but I am continuing *A Tidewater Morning,* which is, in part, a tribute to my father. The story is seen through the eyes of a thirteen-year-old boy, Paul Whitehurst, a Stingo figure, who watches his father almost go mad after the death of his wife, the boy's mother. I may also write a nonfiction piece on depression, after having been hospitalized myself for that illness. Perhaps it will help others.

[Note: Since this interview, Styron did write two articles on depression. See his "Why Primo Levi Need Not Have Died," *The New York Times* (19 December 1988): A17, and "Darkness Visible," *Vanity Fair* (December 1989): 212.]

Works Cited

Bell, Pearl. "Evil and William Styron." *Commentary* (August 1979): 57–59.

Berger, Alan L. *Crisis and Covenant: The Holocaust in American Jewish Fiction*. Albany: State University of New York Press, 1985.

Berger, Joseph. "Witness to Evil: Eliezer Wiesel." *The New York Times* (15 October 1986): A10.

Bettelheim, Bruno. *The Informed Heart*. New York: Avon Books, 1960.

———. "Their Specialty Was Murder." Rev. of *The Nazi Doctors*, by Dr. Robert Jay Lifton. *The New York Times* (5 October 1986), sec. 7:1+.

Blumenthal, Ralph. "No Minor Cases for U. S. Nazi-Hunter." *The New York Times* (16 July 1983): A4.

Camus, Albert. *The Myth of Sisyphus and Other Essays*. Trans. Justin O'Brien. New York: Knopf, 1955.

———. *The Rebel: An Essay on Man in Revolt*. Trans. Anthony Bower. New York: Knopf, 1956.

———. *Resistance, Rebellion, and Death*. Trans. Justin O'Brien. New York: Knopf, 1961.

Caputo, Philip. "Styron's Choices." *Esquire* (December 1986): 136–59.

Chametzky, Jules. *Our Decentralized Literature: Cultural Mediations in Selected Jewish and Southern Writers*. Amherst: University of Massachusetts Press, 1986.

Chiaromonte, Nicola. "Albert Camus: In Memoriam." *Camus: A Collection of Critical Essays*. Ed. Germaine Brée. Englewood Cliffs: Prentice, 1962. 11–15.

Coale, Samuel. "Styron's Disguises: A Provisional Rebel in Christian Masquerade." *Critique* 26.1 (1985): 57–65.

Collins, Glenn. "Women in Nazi Germany: Paradoxes." *The New York Times* (2 March 1987): B6.

Crane, John Kenny. "Looking Down the Barrel of Your Own Gun: William Styron on the Cessation of Warfare." *Delta* 23 (1986): 19–33.

———. *The Root of All Evil: The Thematic Unity of William Styron's Fiction*. Columbia: University of South Carolina Press, 1984.

Dickstein, Morris. "The World in a Mirror: Problems of Distance in Recent American Fiction." *Sewanee* 89 (1981): 386–400.

Durer, Christopher S. "*Moby-Dick* and Nazi Germany." Unpublished essay, 1986.

Ellison, James. "William Styron/A Conversation." *Psychology Today* (January 1983): 27.

Fackenheim, Emil. *To Mend the World*. New York: Schocken Press, 1982.

Freedman, Samuel G. "Games Men Play—On Film and Stage." *The New York Times* (15 March 1987), sec. 2: 30.

Friedlander, Saul. *Reflections of Nazism: An Essay on Kitsch and Death*. Trans. Thomas Weyr. New York: Harper, 1984.

Friedman, Melvin J. "The 'French Face' of William Styron." *The International Fiction Review* 10.1 (1983): 33–37.

Halpern, Daniel. "Checking in with William Styron." *Esquire* (August 1972): 142–43.

Insdorf, Annette. *Indelible Shadows: Film and the Holocaust*. New York: Random, 1983.

Kael, Pauline. "The Current Cinema." *The New Yorker* (27 December 1982): 68 + .

Kreyling, Michael. "Speakable and Unspeakable in Styron's *Sophie's Choice*." *Southern Review* 20 (1984): 546–61.

Lasch, Christopher. *The Minimal Self: Psychic Survival in Troubled Times*. New York: Norton, 1984.

Lifton, Dr. Robert Jay. Letter. *The New York Times* (26 October 1986), sec. 7: 56.

Melville, Herman. *Moby-Dick*. New York: Random, 1930.

Miller, Alice. *For Your Own Good: Hidden Cruelty in Child-Rearing and the Roots of Violence*. New York: Farrar, 1983.

Nordland, Rod. "Death Camps in Every Village." Rev. of *Haing Ngor*, by Haing Ngor with Roger Warner. *The New York Times* (21 February 1988), sec. 7: 30.

Ozick, Cynthia. "A Liberal's Auschwitz." *The Pushcart Prize: Best of the Small Presses*. Ed. Bill Henderson. New York: Pushcart Book Press, 1976. 149–53.

Reynolds, David S. *Beneath the American Renaissance: The Subversive Imagination in the Age of Emerson and Melville*. New York: Knopf, 1988.

Roth, Philip. "A Talk with Aharon Appelfeld." *The New York Times* (28 February 1988), sec. 7: 1 + .

Ruderman, Judith. *William Styron*. New York: Ungar, 1987.

Saposnik, Irving S. "Bellow, Malamud, Roth . . . and Styron? or One Jewish Writer's Response." *Judaism* 31.1 (1982): 322–32.

Seeskin, Kenneth. "Coming to Terms with Failure: A Philosophical Dilemma." In *Writing and the Holocaust*. Ed. Berel Lang. New York: Holmes and Meier, 1988.

"Sevareid Assails TV News." *The New York Times* (25 February 1988): C30.

Simpson, Eileen. *Orphans: Real and Imaginary*. New York: Weidenfeld & Nicholson, 1987.

Steinem, Gloria. "Night Thoughts of a Media Watcher." *Ms.* (November 1981): 22 + .

Steiner, George. *Language and Silence: Essays on Language, Literature and the Inhuman*. New York: Atheneum, 1972.

Stern, Frederick C. "Styron's Choice." *The South Atlantic Quarterly* 82.1 (1983): 19–27.

Styron, William. "Jimmy in the House." *The New York Times* (20 December 1987), sec. 7: 30.

———. *Set This House on Fire*. New York: Random, 1960.

———. *Sophie's Choice*. New York: Random, 1979.

———. *This Quiet Dust and Other Writings*. New York: Random, 1982.

———. "Why Primo Levi Need Not Have Died." *The New York Times* (19 December 1988): A17.

Styron, William, and Candice Bergen. "A Conversation." *Esquire* (January 1982): 86–93.

Thurman, Judith. "William Styron: An Interview." *Mademoiselle* (February 1983): 159 + .

Trouard, Dawn. "Styron's Historical Pre-Text: Nat Turner, Sophie, and the Beginnings of a Postmodern Career." *Papers on Language and Literature* 23.4 (1987): 489–97.

West, James L. W., III, ed. *Conversations with William Styron*. Jackson: University Press of Mississippi, 1985.

Whicher, Stephen E., ed. *Selections from Ralph Waldo Emerson*. Boston: Houghton, 1957.

Wiesel, Elie. "Art and the Holocaust: Trivializing Memory." *The New York Times* (11 June 1989), sec. 2: 1 + .

Index

Fictional characters are alphabetized by first name.